Each recipe includes information on:

– the **number of people** the recipes are intended to serve
– the **preparation and cooking time,** this includes work and cooking or
  baking times
– the **nutritional value** per portion

The following symbols and abbreviations are used:

■   = fairly simple
■■   = somewhat more time-consuming (more complicated)
■■■   = demanding

kcal   = kilocalories (1 kcal=4.184 kJ)
P   = protein
F   = fat
C   = carbohydrate

NB.   1g of protein contains about 4 kcal
             1g of fat contains about 9 kcal
             1g of carbohydrate contains about 4 kcal

All weights and measures in the book are given first in metric, then in
imperial. For example: 100g/4oz or 600ml/1 pint. Always stick to the
same type of measures, metric or imperial, when cooking the recipes.

g   = gram(s)
l   = litre(s)
ml   = millilitre(s)
tbsp   = tablespoon (about 15g/½oz)
tsp   = teaspoon (about 5g/⅙oz)

All temperatures are given for a conventional electric oven, with standard
heating elements. The temperatures correspond to the following gas oven
settings:

175-200°C/350-400°F   = **Gas Mark 1-2**
200-225°C/400-425°F   = **Gas Mark 3-4**
225-250°C/425-475°F   = **Gas Mark 5-6**

– If you are using a fan-assisted oven, the oven temperatures should be
  set 30°C lower than those given conventionally.

– Times and power information for microwave ovens are given
  individually in all microwave recipes.

VERSATILE
VEGETABLES

AUTHORS AND PHOTOGRAPHERS

AN INTRODUCTION TO VEGETABLES

– Friedrich W. Ehlert –
– Odette Teubner, Kerstin Mosny –

HEARTY HOME COOKING

– Rotraud Degner –
– Pete Eising –

DISHES FROM AROUND THE WORLD

– Rotraud Degner –
– Ulrich Kerth –

COOKING FOR SPECIAL OCCASIONS

– Marianne Kaltenbach –
– Rolf Feuz –

WHOLEFOOD RECIPES

– Doris Katharina Hessler –
– Ansgar Pudenz –

QUICK-AND-EASY RECIPES

– Cornelia Adam –
– Michael Brauner –

MICROWAVE RECIPES

– Monika Kellermann –
– Odette Teubner, Kerstin Mosny –

LEAN CUISINE

– Monika Kellermann –
– Anschlag & Goldmann –

Translated by UPS Translations, London
Edition edited by Josephine Bacon and Ros Cocks

CLB 4215
Published originally under the title "Das Neue Menu: Gemüse" by Mosaik
Verlag GmbH, Munich
© Mosaik Verlag, Munich
Project co-ordinator: Peter Schmoeckel
Editors: Ulla Jacobs, Cornella Klaeger, Heidrun Schaaf, Dr Renate Zeltner
Layout: Peter Pleischl, Paul Wollweber

This edition published in 1995 by Grange Books
an imprint of Grange Books PLC,
The Grange, Grange Yard, London, SE1 3AG
English translation copyright © 1995 by CLB Publishing, Godalming, Surrey
Typeset by Image Setting, Brighton, E. Sussex
Printed and Bound in Singapore
ISBN 1-85627-736-4

VERSATILE VEGETABLES

Grange BOOKS

Contents

 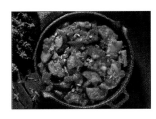  

An Introduction to Vegetables

Whether as a side dish, a main course or an ingredient in soups and stews, vegetables enhance the taste, appearance and nutritional value of any meal. Although the roots, stems, leaves and fruit of plants – which is precisely what vegetables are – used to be boiled to a soft pulp, we now know that the best way to cook vegetables is exactly the opposite. Vegetables that have been conservatively cooked – simmered in a minimum of water – so that they are still firm and crunchy, retain more vitamins and minerals, as well as tasting much better than vegetables which have been boiled until mushy. There are innumerable types of vegetable and just as many ways of preparing them – many of which are presented in this book.

VEGETABLES

Vegetables are low in calories, as well as being rich in valuable substances. All vegetables contain vitamins A (carotin), C and B2, minerals such as potassium, magnesium, calcium, iron and phosphorous, and roughage.

However, the amount and combination of minerals and vitamins varies from one vegetable to another, and they vary according to the amount of light, heat and oxygen to which it has been exposed. Vegetables lying in a bowl, exposed to the light and at room temperature gradually lose their nutritional value. For this reason, vegetables should always be kept cool and in the dark.

TYPES OF VEGETABLE

The almost unimaginable variety of vegetables can be divided into root vegetables, tuberous vegetables, fruit vegetables, leaf vegetables, shoot and stalk vegetables, bulb vegetables and pulses. Root and tuberous vegetables include potatoes, carrots, radishes, turnips and swedes. Courgettes, aubergines, tomatoes and peppers represent fruit vegetables, while all types of green salad and kale, spinach and spinach beet are examples of leaf vegetables. Asparagus, celery, kohlrabi and fennel, as well as other types of vegetables, belong to the group of shoot and stalk vegetables. All types of onion and garlic are combined in the group of bulbous vegetables. Finally, beans, peas and lentils are pulses. Mushrooms belong to a separate group of plants and are not technically vegetables because fungi, of which mushrooms are a species, are

cryptogams or non-flowering plants.

The classification of vegetables according to the time of year when they are harvested is handy when buying vegetables. Spring vegetables are the first vegetables marketed in that year, for example spring onions, early carrots, turnips, asparagus and spinach. Artichokes, various fruit vegetables, beans, peas and spinach beet are harvested in summer and are therefore known as summer vegetables. Cauliflower and turnips are typical autumn vegetables. In winter, the vegetables available include kale, chicory, celeriac, Brussels sprouts, beetroot, carrots, leeks and scorzonera – these are known as winter vegetables. However, now that vegetables are marketed world wide, most are available all year round.

A – Z OF VEGETABLES

The following pages provide information such as the nutritional value of artichokes and many other vegetables, what to remember when preparing individual types of vegetable, plus other useful facts. The vegetables are arranged in alphabetical order. However, it is impossible to cover fully the enormous range of vegetables available, since about 40 to 50 types of vegetable are currently available in more than 1000 varieties. This huge range is constantly on the increase, both as regards what is commercially available and varieties that are home-grown.

Artichokes (globe artichokes) are a type of thistle. The green, still unripe flowering head is harvested as a vegetable and has long been an expensive delicacy. In France artichokes were originally seen as suitable vegetables for rich French noblemen.

Artichokes contain vitamins A and B and are rich in calcium and iron. They are very easy to digest and also stimulate the digestive system and the liver and gall bladder functions.

Two types of globe artichoke are generally available: large, round, green artichokes with a fleshy base, which are cultivated in Brittany; and small, purple ones with pointed leaves, from Italy and Spain.

Usually only the base and the fleshy part of the leaves are eaten. This is just 20% of the flower head! However, the tender, fresh stalks, when peeled and boiled, make excellent vegetables and are good in salads.

Artichokes should not be cooked in aluminium or iron saucepans, since they will colour them greyish-black.

Storage: about 3 days in the vegetable compartment of the refrigerator.

Asparagus is in season from mid-April to late June.

Green asparagus is favoured in Britain, but white (blanched) asparagus has long been known as the king of vegetables in central Europe, especially Germany and Austria. Large asparagus spears are expensive, but the thinner grades, especially the almost grass-like one known as sprue, are cheaper.

Asparagus is extremely low in calories (17 kcal per 100g) and contains protein, roughage, and various vitamins and minerals. Its characteristic flavour is derived from volatile oils, vanillin and other chemical compounds. Green asparagus takes its colour from the green pigment chlorophyll, and has a higher vitamin content than white asparagus. In contrast to white asparagus, it should not be peeled, though the lower ends may need scraping.

In addition to green and white asparagus, stronger-flavoured asparagus types with yellow or purple tips from France or the Mediterranean countries are also available. Good-quality fresh asparagus has straight stems of equal diameter. If the cut surfaces are scratched they should produce juice.

Storage: 2-3 days wrapped in a damp cloth in the vegetable compartment of the refrigerator. But whenever possible asparagus should be used fresh.

Aubergines, or egg plants, belong to the same family as tomatoes, peppers and potatoes. Originally they were white or yellow and about the size of a hen's egg, hence egg plant.

Now the elongated purple type is predominant. The flesh of aubergines contains calcium, iron and vitamins B and C. Aubergines stimulate the liver and gall bladder functions and have a favourable effect on rheumatism.

The flavour of these vegetables is only brought out by boiling, roasting or grilling. Eaten raw, they can cause diarrhoea, vomiting and stomach pains.

There is no need to peel them, especially as the dark colour of the skin is part of their attraction. Aubergine recipes often include instructions for 'degorging' them to remove bitterness, but this is not normally necessary nowadays as they should be nice and fresh when bought. However, if you are particularly sensitive to bitter flavours simply sprinkle the cut surfaces with salt and leave to drain for about 30 minutes. Salting draws the bitterness out of the fruit, but also the water-soluble vitamins and minerals.

Storage: about 5-6 days in the vegetable compartment of the refrigerator.

Broccoli is a member of the cabbage family and is an ancestor of cauliflower. The young flower heads are eaten while still in bud and, in contrast to cauliflower, some of the stalks as well. The delicate cabbage flavour is reminiscent of green asparagus. Compared with other types of cabbage broccoli is easy to digest and therefore suitable as a light food. It contains primarily vitamins A and C, and calcium.

In addition to green broccoli, there are also red, blue and purple types. Calabrese is a variety with extra-large tender greeny-blue heads, available in summer; sprouting broccoli is a winter vegetable producing lots of small spears. If broccoli is blanched before the actual cooking process, the taste is enhanced and the colour retained.

Broccoli should always be prepared fresh. Signs of freshness are a bright colour and tightly closed flowers.

Storage: about 2 days in the vegetable compartment of the refrigerator.

Brussels sprouts are one of the finest representatives of the cabbage family. They are typical winter vegetables, which were first grown more than 100 years ago near Brussels. If Brussels sprouts are to flourish, the autumn must be warm and the winter mild. Sprouts are rich in the minerals potassium, magnesium, iron and phosphorous, as well as vitamins B and C. Frost increases the sugar content of sprouts, which refines the flavour and makes them easier to digest, since the cellulose tissue (cell structure) is loosened.

Good-quality sprouts should be bright green and firm, with no discoloured outer leaves. Avoid small, pale ones: these are stale larger ones which have been trimmed by the greengrocer to make them look saleable.

The individual sprouts cook to a firm consistency in 15 minutes or less, according to their size. Cutting a cross in the base of the stalk is often recommended, but is not necessary unless some are larger than others, to ensure that they all cook at the same rate.

Storage: firmly closed sprouts, 2-3 days in the vegetable compartment of the refrigerator.

Cabbage, whether plain green, savoy or white, is always available and, like red cabbage, is a type of head cabbage.

Cabbage is a valuable foodstuff. In olden times, sailors protected themselves from scurvy, a disease caused by a lack of vitamin C, by eating pickled cabbage (sauerkraut) in addition to the more well-known ration of lime or lemon juice.

Cabbage is still a healthy component of our diets since it is rich in vitamins B1, B2 and C, and in important minerals (iron, magnesium, sodium and phosphorous).

Cabbage is difficult to digest, but can be made more digestible by blanching in hot salted water or by seasoning with caraway seeds. Cabbage heads should be firmly closed.

Spring greens or spring cabbage is a type of cabbage with a conical head. The large green leaves form a loose cone. It has a more delicate structure and flavour than other types, as well as a shorter storage life. Spring greens are small heads of a leafy green cabbage with no heart.

Storage: up to a fortnight in the vegetable compartment of the refrigerator. Always cover cut surfaces with cling film. Spring cabbage – a maximum of 2 days.

PULSES, FRESH AND DRIED

The mature seeds of members of the pea and bean family – pulses – are one of the oldest foodstuffs known. This group includes beans, peas, lentils and soya beans. Pulses contain plenty of roughage, biologically valuable protein, carbohydrates, minerals and B-vitamins. Combined with cereals (as in beans on toast) pulses provide a valuable replacement for meat in our diet.

Fresh peas and beans make the tastiest side dishes, after only a few minutes' cooking.

Beans come in a wide range of colours and sizes, particularly dried, but quite a few are also available canned. Popular ones include reddish flecked borlotti beans (12, 7), red kidney beans (15), reddish-black scarlet runner beans (13), olive green mung beans (17) and reddish-brown aduki beans (14). Both the latter types are suitable for germinating and eating as sprouts. In addition there are black beans, haricot beans, black-eyed beans (also known as black-eyed peas), the delicate pale green flageolets and the most valuable bean of all – the soya bean (16).

Most dried beans and peas require soaking to soften them and reduce the cooking time. Broadly speaking, the larger the bean the longer the soaking time; the exceptions are chick peas and soya beans, which are extremely tough. Lentils do not need soaking. Overnight soaking is often convenient for large or tough beans, but for smaller ones a few hours will suffice, especially if you use boiling water.

Boil the beans in fresh water, quite vigorously at first, then more gently. Do not add salt as this toughens the skins. Cook for as long as needed to make them really tender. Undercooked or improperly cooked beans cause digestive problems and some (red and black kidney beans) can be harmful.

French beans (8) are among the most widely used. Young, tender beans are suitable for use in salads, while the medium-sized ones are used as a vegetable.

Runner beans (6) are climbing plants grown up poles or strings, and so also known as pole beans or string beans. They are usually flat-podded, with quite rough skins, but can also be round-podded. When young they are tender, with good flavour and texture, and can be treated like French beans. But they are commonly sold far too big, when they are coarse and stringy. Such beans must be de-stringed and finely sliced to be edible. Runner beans are mainly used as a vegetable and in soups.

Wax beans (9) or yellow beans are the yellow variety of the French bean. They are very tender and best suited for salads.

Dwarf French beans (10) are very tender, early beans, with a delicate flavour and fine texture. They are divided into three grades – extra, very fine and fine.

Broad beans are not really beans, but are eaten as such; they are also known as fava beans. When dried, the beans are light to dark brown (11).

Unless they are very young, beans should not be eaten raw. In this state, they contain the poisonous substance phasin, which can lead to inflammation and stomach complaints. During cooking this heat-sensitive substance is destroyed. So cooking them requires careful timing to ensure that they are tender but still crisp.

Fresh beans are juicy and evenly green or yellow in colour. They make a sharp cracking sound when broken in the fingers, which is why they are also known as snap beans.

Storage: about 3 days in the vegetable compartment of the refrigerator, in a plastic bag.

Peas are not only delicious in stews and soups, but can also be made into tasty purées. Yellow (3) and green peas (4, 5) and chick peas (2) are the best-known types. Dried peas can be obtained either whole or split. Discoveries in various parts of the world indicate that people ate peas as early as 7000 BC. Until well into the Middle Ages only peas from mature pods were eaten; they were a basic foodstuff as well as a medicine. Then Italian cooks discovered that peas can also be cooked and eaten when green and unripe. Fresh peas in the pod are unfortunately not frequently found in shops, since most are processed for canning or freezing.

Peas are classified according to type and pea size:

Wrinkled peas are sweet and tender, contain mainly carbohydrate as sugar and are almost square.

Round-seeded peas are also known as garden or shelled peas, and are rounded and smooth, with a high starch content, giving them a floury taste.

Mange-tout peas, snow peas or sugar snaps (1) are a special variety of pea, eaten whole when the seeds inside have scarcely developed and the pod is paper-thin and extremely tender. Mange-tout have almost completely flat pods, while the sugar snaps are more rounded. They are increasingly popular, and are very quick to cook.

Peas in the pod. The peas inside are not tough, and although time-consuming to prepare, are well worth the effort, for the flavour of truly fresh peas is unsurpassed. They can be eaten hot or cold.

The high protein, carbohydrate, vitamin and mineral content of peas makes them a nutritious food. Small, fresh, crisp peas are always the best. The same applies to mange-tout peas. Dried peas, by contrast, should be large.

Storage: 1-2 days in the vegetable compartment of the refrigerator. The boiling time should be doubled after one day's storage!

Lentils have been grown in Asia for millennia and today are grown mainly in India and Turkey. The greenish-brown or Puy lentils (20), black (18) and orange or Egyptian lentils (19) are only available dried, either whole or split. As with all pulses, the cross-section determines the price. The smaller and therefore better-value types are of course the most tasty. Red or Egyptian lentils have the best flavour of all, and these are usually sold split. They do not take as long to cook as brown lentils.

Soya beans (16) are extremely high in protein and have far and away the highest fat content of all pulses – 100 grams of soya beans contain 18 grams of fat. The whole beans are always eaten dried; they have little flavour and take a long time to cook. However, they can be used in many other ways, and as a result of their versatility the area cultivated for soya beans is increasing all over the world. Soya beans are used to make soya oil, lecithin, soya meal and soya flour, protein concentrate, soya milk, tofu (bean curd) and soy sauce.

Carrots come in two types – short, rounded ones and long, pointed ones. Carrots are an extremely old variety of vegetable, which have been eaten for a good 5000 to 6000 years in central Europe.

They are one of the most popular and frequently used vegetables and contain the most carotin (provitamin A) of all. Carotin is only absorbed by the body in combination with fat. Minerals, vitamins C and E, few calories and easy digestibility make carrots a much-loved ingredient in our diet. They have a sweetish, nutty flavour, as a result of their high fructose content. Young carrots do not require peeling, only scraping or scrubbing, as preferred.

Early carrots are smaller varieties which have not overwintered. They are about the length and thickness of a finger and are usually sold in bunches with the leaves. They have a sweet, delicate flavour.

Summer carrots are sold from about June to September. They are larger than early carrots.

Late carrots are suitable for storing. They are available from November to March.

Storage: about 3-4 weeks, ventilated and kept cool in a dark place or in the vegetable compartment of the refrigerator.

Cauliflower is one of the few types of vegetable from which the flower head or inflorescence is eaten. It has a delicately pronounced cabbage flavour which is easily lost through over-cooking, and is best steamed or boiled whole rather than cut into florets.

Its delicate cell structure and relatively high vitamin C and calcium contents endow the cauliflower with its nutritional value. The Romans and Greeks prized cauliflower, not only for its taste. Various healing powers were also attributed to it.

Cauliflower is available in various types. In addition to the well-known white cauliflower, there are also green (romanesco) and purple types. Firm, closed heads are the mark of freshness of this vegetable.

Storage: 3-5 days in the vegetable compartment of the refrigerator.

Celeriac looks like a large, misshapen turnip root but tastes strongly of celery. It is actually a swollen stem that grows above ground. Although not as popular in Britain as it is in central Europe it can be found during the winter months. It is used in a similar way to celery, makes a flavoursome addition to soups and stews, and can also be eaten raw in salads. To prepare celeriac, which is often very knobbly, cut it into thick slices, then peel each slice. Stack the slices and cut them into strips, then into dice. Using plenty of celeriac means using less salt. If lemon juice is added to the water it remains white when boiled.

Storage: about 8 days in the vegetable compartment of the refrigerator.

Celery is available all year round in two basic varieties, white and green. The fleshy stalks are rich in Vitamin C and also contain an extremely large amount of potassium. Fresh celery has crisp stalks and green leaves. Because of its crunchiness celery is very good raw, especially with cheese; when cooked the flavour intensifies and it is eaten as a vegetable or added to stews and soups.

Storage: 1-2 weeks in the vegetable compartment of the refrigerator, kept in its plastic sleeve.

Chard (also known as Swiss Chard or Silverbeet) is an unusual vegetable, a member of the beet family, grown mainly for the large thick stems or ribs, ending in rather coarse green leaves. The common variety has creamy white stems, but there is also one with red stems, known as ruby or rhubarb chard.

Chard is rich in protein and is made up of a combination of substances similar to those of spinach. It contains primarily the minerals phosphorous, potassium, calcium, magnesium, iron, iodine and vitamins B1, B2 and C. Chard is recognised as a medicinal plant as a result of its laxative properties and its sedative effects. The stems and leaves are cooked separately. The chopped or cut stems are steamed, braised or boiled, and best served on their own as they have a delicate flavour reminiscent of asparagus. The leaves are cooked in the same way as spinach.

Storage: in the vegetable compartment of the refrigerator. In a plastic bag, the leaves keep for 2-3 days. Wrapped in damp paper, the stems keep for about 8 days.

Chicory is a close relative of witloof chicory, or Belgian endive. It was discovered accidentally at the end of the 19th century by Belgian farmers, who found that when grown in the dark it develops strong, pale shoots – chicory. Today, Belgium is still the main source of chicory, and Brussels witloof is synonymous with quality. Chicory is grown underground or under black polythene so that it stays tender and pale.

Chicory has a bittersweet flavour which not everyone appreciates, but it is rich in vitamins and minerals. In addition, it is considered good for diabetics and people suffering from rheumatism. Radicchio is the Italian name given to the red variety of chicory.

When buying chicory make sure that it is tightly closed and pale.

Storage: about 4-5 days in the vegetable compartment of the refrigerator, wrapped in damp paper. If kept out too long the leaves turn light green and the bitter taste becomes stronger.

Corn on the cob is not a vegetable, but a cereal grain (maize), which originally comes from America and was introduced to Europe by Christopher Columbus. The tender, pale golden niblets of sweetcorn are used as a vegetable. Corn contains valuable protein, little fat and a lot of carbohydrate, in the form of starch. In addition, it also contains vitamins from the B group (particularly niacin) and potassium.

Sweetcorn is the term used to refer to corn off the cob, almost always canned or frozen. It is one of America's favourite vegetables and is also increasing in popularity in Europe.

Corn cobs are harvested when unripe, as soon as the niblets have developed and are juicy. The cob is broken from the stem during harvesting and sold in its leafy shell. Look for cobs with pale gold niblets – if they are dark, the corn was too old when picked and will be tough. Baby sweetcorn, harvested when immature, is a popular ingredient in Oriental cooking, but has little flavour.

Corn cobs should be boiled for 5-8 minutes in slightly sweetened water, without salt, which stops them from hardening.

Storage: fresh corn keeps for a few days in the vegetable compartment of the refrigerator.

Courgettes or zucchini belong to the gourd or squash family and are a type of baby marrow. They come originally from America where they have been grown for over 6000 years. Courgettes, together with avocados and chillies, are among the oldest cultivated plants.

'Zucchino' is the diminutive form of the Italian word 'zucca', meaning gourd. Courgettes are harvested when unripe and only 15-20 cm (6-8 in) long; at this stage they have no seeds in the centre. They are usually dark green but there are also types which are flecked or striped white, entirely white, yellow and golden. Young, tender courgettes do not have to be peeled, but some people find the skin of larger ones slightly bitter. They are boiled or fried in vegetable dishes, and can also be added raw to salads. Even the yellow courgette flowers are enjoying increasing popularity in our kitchens.

Like all gourd vegetables, courgettes contain a great deal of water, are low in calories, rich in vitamins and easy to digest.

Storage: 3-4 days in the vegetable compartment of the refrigerator or other cool place.

Cucumber is one of the oldest cultivated plants. It is said to have been grown in India in 4000 BC. In the Middle Ages it became known in southern, central and northern Europe.

Long, thin salad cucumbers and fatter, cylindrical ridge cucumbers are suitable in salads and as a vegetable. After sorting according to size, immature, smaller pickling cucumbers are industrially processed into fine-quality gherkins and pickled gherkins. The smallest are known as cornichons. Both outdoor and greenhouse cucumbers are available on the market. Outdoor cucumbers have a stronger flavour. Cucumbers are extremely low in calories as they consist almost entirely of water, and are rich in vitamins and minerals. Look for cucumbers that are firm, especially at the stalk end. Do not peel unless it is essential to the recipe, as most of the food value lies in the skin.

Storage: 6-7 days in the vegetable compartment of the refrigerator.

Fennel should really be called bulb fennel, to distinguish it from the green leafy tops. While fennel bulbs have been valued for a long time in southern Europe, particularly in Italy, both as a vegetable and in salads, they have been slow to catch on over here. They have a distinct taste of aniseed and go particularly well with fish.

There are two types of bulb fennel – Florence fennel, which has a narrow, elongated bulb and a delicate flavour, and Italian fennel, which has a firm, thick bulb and a more pronounced flavour. Fennel contains essential oils which are responsible for its typical flavour, as well as minerals and vitamins C and E. Once sliced, fennel should be sprinkled immediately with lemon juice to maintain its whiteness. It can be eaten raw or cooked and goes well with tomatoes, courgettes and aubergines.

Storage: at least 14 days in the vegetable compartment of the refrigerator.

Kale is a member of the cabbage family with loose curly green leaves, which was enjoyed as a vegetable in the winter months even before Roman times. It actually comes from the countries around the Mediterranean Sea. Kale is very hardy and only develops its full flavour after the first frosts. For this reason freezing actually improves the quality of this vegetable, both in terms of taste and nutritional value. Frost breaks down its starch content into sugar, which makes it easier to digest. It contains a great deal of calcium, vitamin A (carotin) and vitamin C. A kilogram of freshly cut kale contains one gram of vitamin C – a vitamin content surpassed only by Brussels sprouts. Kale matches spinach in terms of its mineral content. Fresh kale can be recognised by its stiff green leaves.

Kale can be made into an especially hearty dish if braised together with loin of pork, pork sausage and smoked bacon.

Storage: 2-3 days in the vegetable compartment of the refrigerator.

Kohlrabi is probably descended from the cabbage eaten in Pompeii by the Romans and was first grown in Europe as early as the 16th century. It is a member of the cabbage family, and is sometimes called turnip-cabbage but differs from other types in that the round root is eaten and the leaves are usually cut away. Kohlrabi comes in various shapes and colours: rounded or flattened, from almost white, through greenish-white to purple. The colour reveals the origin of the kohlrabi. The white variety is usually grown in greenhouses, while the red is grown outdoors. Both varieties have white flesh. Greenhouse kohlrabi has a more delicate structure and taste, while outdoor kohlrabi has a stronger flavour.

Kohlrabi is rich in vitamin C and minerals such as calcium, potassium, phosphorous, magnesium, iron and sodium. Young kohlrabi are particularly suitable for vegetable dishes and salads. The leaves, if present, contain a great deal of carotin (provitamin A) and should be used chopped in vegetable dishes or salads.

Storage: 2 days if kept cool and moist. Kohlrabi becomes woody if stored longer than this.

Leeks form part of the extensive onion family and are used as vegetables, for flavouring and in soups and salads. They are extremely rich in valuable substances, particularly iron, carotin (provitamin A) and vitamins B1, B2, C and E, and contain the appetite-stimulating sulphurous leek oil, which is responsible for the typical leek smell.

Leeks can be divided into three groups:

Early leeks are tender and mild, with pale green foliage and a white stalk. They are highly suitable for use as vegetables, in soups and as a flavouring. They are also suitable for eating raw with mixed raw vegetables and in salads.

Summer leeks have thin skins and a long white, fairly strong stalk, with green foliage. They are delicious eaten as a cooked vegetable.

Winter leeks have green/blue foliage and a strong, short stalk. The foliage has a strong flavour, while the stalk is mild and delicate. In winter, blanched leeks are also available. Their white colour is caused by the lack of light. The soil is heaped up around the stalks, which also makes them hard.

Storage: 10-12 days in the vegetable compartment of the refrigerator.

Onions are indispensable in cooking, both as a flavouring and a vegetable. In addition to vitamins A and C, they also contain minerals such as potassium and magnesium, and they have an antibacterial effect.

The following types of onion are sold:

The brown onion, which has the strongest flavour, is the most common; the colour of the flesh ranges from white to yellow.

The Spanish onion is the largest and mildest. Its flesh is juicy and is suitable for eating raw in salads or with bread and cheese, roasting, baking, stuffing and boiling.

The spring onion is a miniature variety picked when the bulbs are barely developed. It is eaten raw in salads and is an important component of Chinese cooking. The green tops are a good substitute for chives.

The red or salad onion has a spicy but mild flavour compared with the common brown onion. It is good in salads, and can be used in cooked dishes.

Shallots, the smallest and finest representatives of the onion family, are very popular in French cuisine. They have a very delicate flavour and are used in classic sauces, regional dishes and salads.

Storage: several weeks if kept cool and dry.

Peas: see Pulses

Peppers should actually be referred to as sweet peppers, bell peppers or capsicums to distinguish them from their much hotter relative the chilli pepper. The most commonly available are bell shaped and green, red, yellow or black. In addition to carbohydrate and protein, they contain important minerals and vitamins, including ten times more vitamin C than lemons. The white cores and membranes contain capsaicin, which gives peppers their spicy flavour.

Hot peppers or chillies are also members of the capsicum family, but are much smaller and slimmer. They originate in Mexico, where endless different varieties are used, with varying degrees of hotness. Green chillies are generally hotter than red (ripe) ones. They are used whenever a hot taste is required in a dish, notably in chilli con carne, and to make cayenne pepper and paprika. When preparing chillies, wash hands and equipment thoroughly afterwards, and be very careful not to get the juice in your eyes via your fingers; it stings. If fresh chillies are not available dried ones are a good substitute.

Storage: 3-5 days in the vegetable compartment of the refrigerator.

Red cabbage is a type of head cabbage and has been enjoyed as a vegetable since the 8th century. It differs from other head cabbages in that it has a higher vitamin C content. In addition, it is easier to digest, contains more roughage and is – naturally – red. Its reddish blue leaves turn a deeper red with the addition of acid, which is why most recipes for cooking it include a little vinegar, wine, lemon juice or cooking apple. It associates especially well with pork and game. Red cabbage should never be boiled in an aluminium saucepan, because the red dye reacts with aluminium and loses its strength and the cabbage turns a blueish colour. Red cabbage is available almost all year round, as early cabbage, semi-early cabbage and autumn cabbage.

Storage: up to 14 days in the vegetable compartment of the refrigerator. Always cover a cut cabbage with foil.

Savoy cabbage is another major type of cabbage, in addition to the green and red varieties. It comes from the northern Mediterranean area and was cooked as long ago as the Middle Ages.

Savoy cabbage is not as tightly closed as red and green cabbage types. Its leaves are wrinkled and curly. It comes in many types and colours, from dark green to yellow. The dark green early Savoy cabbage is the most valued variety. In addition to the early variety, Savoy cabbage is also available in autumn and winter varieties. Savoy cabbage keeps the least well of all cabbage types. It is cooked in the same way as the other types and goes well with game and lamb.

Dark green Savoy cabbage contains more valuable nutrients than white cabbage and is also easier to digest.

Storage: about 14 days in the vegetable compartment of the refrigerator.

Scorzonera (black salsify or oyster plant) is relatively uncommon in Britain, although very popular in Europe. It is a winter root vegetable which has been cultivated since the 17th century. Its wild form, which is native in southern Europe, had already been in use as a medicinal plant for a long time. Scorzonera is highly nutritious, mainly as a result of its carbohydrate, mineral (potassium, calcium, phosphorous and iron) and vitamin contents. Its inulin content is particularly noteworthy. This is a carbohydrate made from fructose which is suitable for diabetics. When peeled, scorzonera produces a milky juice that darkens the skin, so wear gloves. It also discolours rapidly after peeling, but this can be prevented by immediately putting each root into water with a little vinegar added. When buying scorzonera make sure the surface is smooth and the flesh pale and juicy.
Storage: 14 days in the vegetable compartment of the refrigerator, wrapped in paper.

Spinach is notable for its relatively high iron content in comparison with other vegetables. Many vegetable types contain between 1 and 3 milligrams of iron per 100 grams, but spinach contains over 4 milligrams per 100 grams.
By contrast, it should be noted that spinach is high in nitrates, which are further increased by the use of chemical fertilisers. Oxygen (air) and heat convert nitrates into poisonous nitrites, which are particularly harmful to children. For this reason, spinach should only be used fresh (without being stored) and should not be reheated. The nitrate level can also be reduced by thorough washing. Cook while still wet without adding any extra water; cover the pan and shake it from time to time. Spinach cooks down tremendously, so buy at least 250g/8oz per person. Fresh spinach should be crisp and dark green.
Spinach beet looks very similar to spinach and is often sold as such, but it is actually a completely different plant, related to beetroot but grown for the leaves rather than the root. The leaves are larger and the stems coarser; remove these when washing. Otherwise treat exactly like spinach.
Storage: not recommended.

Tomatoes were first grown in Italy and in the south-eastern Mediterranean area. Tomatoes are rich in minerals and vitamins, especially vitamin C. Round tomatoes account for the largest market share. They are suitable for both cooking and salads Their sweet-and-sour flavour can be enhanced by adding a pinch of sugar. Green parts, which should always be removed before eating, indicate the presence of the toxic substance solanine.
Beefsteak tomatoes are large, with a very fruity flavour and a high proportion of meaty flesh. They are best enjoyed raw but can also be used in hot dishes.
Plum tomatoes are named for their shape, and are the ones peeled and canned in great quantities. They have an excellent flavour but this only develops with cooking, so they are not at their best in salads, although very firm and with a deep red colour. The canned ones are excellent for use in made-up dishes.
Cherry tomatoes are a relative novelty. These mini-tomatoes have a fruity flavour and are ideal for garnishing and salads.
Storage: several days at room temperature, longer in the refrigerator.

Turnips come in various shapes and sizes and used to be extremely widespread, but have now been displaced by the potato. During periods of crisis and in wartime they have always experienced an upswing in consumption. Most turnips do not contain any substance of note, but all types are low in calories.
Baby or white turnips are the first of the year, with a white skin, white flesh and a sweetish flavour. They taste best when they are about the size of a hen's egg, and do not need peeling.
Navets or french turnips are a small variety, rather flattened, with pale purple and white skins which should be left on. The flavour is delicate, rather like that of kohlrabi.
Late turnips are larger than baby turnips, with white flesh and a sharp flavour. They are good with lamb and pork.
Swedes or rutabaga are larger than turnips, greenish-yellow or purplish-yellow on the outside, and with pale orange flesh on the inside. They are a good winter vegetable, suitable for use in stews and soups. They are also delicious cooked and mashed with plenty of butter and pepper. In northern parts of Britain they are known as turnips or neeps.
Storage: about 1 week in the vegetable compartment of the refrigerator.

POTATOES

Potatoes are one of our major basic foodstuffs. They originated in the central highlands and coastal area of the Andes. In the 16th century, sailors brought this nondescript tuber to Europe, via a circuitous route. Today, nutritious and vitamin-rich potatoes are indispensable in our cuisine. The starchy tubers contain a relatively large amount of calcium, iron, potassium, sodium and phosphorous, vitamins A, B1, B2 and C. Green potatoes contain the toxin solanine and for this reason should not be eaten.

The range of possibilities for using potatoes is enormous. Whether boiled or steamed, roasted or baked, fried or chipped, made into gratins, soups or stews, they always taste good!

TYPES

There are currently between 100 and 120 types of potato, only a few of which are marketed. They are subdivided as follows:

Earlies: available May-July. Usually sold as new potatoes for immediate use.

Second earlies: available August-March. Can be stored for a short time.

Maincrop: available from September-May. Suitable for storing in a frost-free dark place.

TEXTURE

Potatoes are not only classified according to type, but also according to their texture once cooked, which is determined by their starch content. The earlier the potatoes ripen, the less starch they contain and the firmer they are when cooked. Only the older types accumulate so much starch during the

SUMMARY OF COOKING TYPE AND STORAGE LIFE OF SOME POPULAR TYPES OF POTATO

Types	Cooking characteristics	Storage
earlies (scrapers)		
Maris Bard	soft waxy texture	intended for immediate
Pentland Javelin	soft waxy texture	use after harversting
Rocket	firm waxy texture	
second earlies		
Estima	firm, moist texture	can be stored for a few
Wilja	firm, slightly dry texture	weeks if kept cool and dark
maincrop		
Desirée	firm texture	suitable for long storage
Maris Piper	floury texture	suitable for long storage
King Edward	floury texture	suitable for long storage
Romano	soft dry texture	suitable for long storage

sunny summer months that they become light and floury when cooked. All the available types of potato fall into one of three cooking categories (see table). Buy from good shops where the varieties are properly labelled, so that you can be sure they will be suitable for your purpose.

Waxy potatoes have a low starch content and do not fall apart when cooked. They are firm and should be used for potato salads, unpeeled boiled potatoes and plain boiled potatoes.Examples are Jersey Royal, Maris Bard, Pink Fir Apple, Pentland Javelin, Rocket.

All-purpose potatoes have an average starch content. They remain firm when cooked and are slightly floury. During boiling, the skins split open. Some are mainly waxy and suitable for potato salads and for unpeeled boiled potatoes, but most are good all-rounders, used for roasting, boiling, chipping and baking. Examples are Cara, Desirée, Estima, Maris Piper, Pentland Dell, Wilja.

Floury potatoes have a high starch content. After cooking, they are floury, dry and light. They also tend to be large, and are ideal for mashing and baking. Examples are King Edward, Pentland Squire, Romano.

STORAGE

Smaller quantities of potatoes should be kept cool, if possible in the dark and ventilated (preferably in a cardboard box). Carefully remove all plastic packaging. Do not put potatoes in the refrigerator, where they will quickly go off. If storing larger quantities for a longer period, or putting them in a cellar or outhouse, bear in mind the following:

Potatoes for storing must be fully ripe with a firm, undamaged skin; if possible they should be clean. On no account should the potatoes be washed before storing. A thin layer of dry soil on the skin does no harm and even provides protection against rotting. The ideal storage temperature is around 4°C/ 40°F. Cool, dry, dark cellars

or store-rooms make good storage places, but they must always be frost-free and well ventilated. Frost eventually converts the starch into sugar and gives the potatoes a slightly sweet taste. Adequate ventilation, particularly from below, is important. Paper sacks or plastic mesh bags are suitable, but they should not be piled higher than 40cm/16 inches. Never store in polythene bags. If the potatoes are not in paper sacks it is worth loosely covering them with newspaper since light can cause green patches to form, which contain toxic solanine (all patches must be cut out before cooking). Sprouting potatoes should be used quickly; remove the sprouts before cooking.

MUSHROOMS

Mushrooms may well be used as vegetables, but they are fungi. They form an individual, large botanical group.

In terms of nutritional value, edible mushrooms are similar to vegetables. In terms of minerals, they contain primarily potassium and phosphorous. They also contain vitamin D, which only occurs very rarely in vegetables. Since the cell walls of mushrooms contain chitin and cellulose, they are difficult to digest. Even mushroom protein is relatively difficult to digest and is poorly absorbed by the body.

Ordinary closed cup or button mushrooms are often the only type available. But other types are slowly coming onto the market, and the following are the most likely to be found:

Birch boletus (4) are closely related to the cep and are associated mainly with birch trees. They have white flesh which quickly discolours and yellow pores. As soon as the cap and stalk have been cut, it becomes deep red to violet in colour. These wild fungi have an aromatic flavour and go well with game dishes.

Boletus luteus (8) is a close relative of the cep (Boletus edulis), but is not often offered for sale in Britain. It has white, butter-soft flesh. The slimy brown skin of the cap can easily be removed.

Storage: this mushroom goes off quickly and should be used immediately.

Ceps or penny buns (10) grow in deciduous and coniferous forests. The cap of young mushrooms is light brown and semi-spherical. Older ones have red to dark brown, parasol-like caps. Thanks to their nutty flavour, ceps have a wide variety of uses; they are widely used in the production of canned and packeted soups. They are also suitable for use raw in salads.

Storage: use immediately. Dried mushrooms should be soaked in cold water for a little while before use.

Chanterelles (9). These bright yellow edible mushrooms with funnel-shaped caps grow in deciduous and coniferous forests. They can be prepared almost without waste and are suitable as an accompaniment to game dishes, egg dishes or as a flavouring for sauces.

Storage: fresh mushrooms can be kept for one or two days in the vegetable compartment of the refrigerator or in a cool, dark place. Chanterelles become very hard if allowed to dry out and are less suitable for deep-frying, since this gives them a bitter taste.

Closed cup (1, 3) or brown mushrooms (2) are the best known and most widely used edible mushrooms. They are always available. The caps of young mushrooms are still firmly closed and have grown with the stalk. The cap gradually opens as the mushroom ages and the colour of the originally pale gills changes to dark brown, via dark pink. The progressive stages are known as button, closed cup, open cup and flat. Fresh button or closed cup mushrooms should be firm and crisp. If the stalk ends are dark, this indicates that the mushrooms have been stored for some time. Button mushrooms are ideal for cooking whole, or for use in creamy sauces, as the pale gills cause no discolouration. Closed cup mushrooms are extremely versatile and can be fried, braised, stewed or grilled and are especially tasty used raw in salads. Open cup mushrooms are good for frying, stuffing and baking; flat mushrooms are only suitable for use in stews and mushroom soup as they impart a dark colour; but they have the best flavour. Brown mushrooms, sometimes labelled chestnut mushrooms, have a stronger flavour than the white types, but are not so widely available.

These mushrooms are grown in clean conditions and do not need peeling or washing, just wiping with absorbent paper.

Storage: mushrooms pre-packaged in film should be removed from the packaging after purchase. If the mushrooms are fresh, firm and not too damp, they will stay fresh in the vegetable compartment of the refrigerator for a few days. Closed cup mushrooms which have dried during storage can still be used if soaked in milk for a little while before cooking.

Morels (6) are some of the most strongly flavoured edible mushrooms of the genus Morchella. The stalk is wrinkled and hollow, the cap is pitted and honeycomb-like. Depending on the shape of the cap, a distinction is made between round and pointed morels. Since fresh morels are very sandy, they must be thoroughly washed before use. Dried morels need to be soaked for 2 hours, after which they still have to be washed. Morels are used more as flavouring than as an edible mushroom.

Storage: use as fresh as possible. These mushrooms should not be stored.

Oyster mushrooms (5) or oyster fungus. The cap ranges from 5cm/¼ inch to 15cm/ 6 inches across, is rounded or semi-circular and varying in colour from grey/mauve and blueish-grey to olive/black. There are also yellow to brownish types. Oyster mushrooms are mildly aromatic with a delicate flavour. When bought they should feel firm and robust, and small to medium ones are preferable to larger ones. In addition to their many uses as a side dish or flavouring, the caps can also be breaded and fried like escalopes of meat. They are often used in Oriental cuisine.

Storage: if not used immediately, they are best stored in the refrigerator, preferably in the vegetable compartment, or in a cool, dark place for a further 2 to 3 days. Dried ones should be soaked briefly in hot water.

Shiitake mushrooms (7) came originally from Japan, where they have been cultivated for many centuries. They have been commercially available for only a short time but are gaining in popularity due to their strong spicy flavour and pronounced aroma. The mushrooms have a slightly ribbed, pale to dark brown cap, covered in pale scales. If it is fresh, the cap should be cupped. Shiitake mushrooms are mainly suitable in Oriental cuisine, particularly stews.

Storage: will stay fresh for a few days if stored loosely in a cool, dark place.

Truffles (11, 12) are bulbous fungi, covered in a rough skin. They have firm flesh. Specially trained dogs or pigs are sometimes used to find these fungi, which grow underground. The best black truffles come from southern France (Périgord truffles). They are best when cooked in champagne or Madeira. The best white truffles come from northern Italy (Piedmont truffles) and are usually sliced wafer-thin, raw, over food, as they are incredibly expensive.

TIPS FOR BUYING VEGETABLES

Healthy eating means buying vegetables which are in season at a given time of year, because artificial after-ripening and long transportation reduce the levels of valuable ingredients in vegetables. In addition, greenhouse vegetables contain a higher level of harmful chemicals (fertiliser residues and nitrates) than vegetables grown outdoors.

Organically grown vegetables may not be entirely free of harmful substances, but they do contain considerably fewer undesirable substances than conventionally cultivated vegetables.

Although most vegetables are available all year round, some vegetables are most definitely seasonal. Since vegetable growing is dependent on the weather, changes in the times shown on the vegetable calendar cannot be ruled out. When buying vegetables, fresh ones are not always available. In this case, frozen vegetables are recommended as an alternative. Vegetables can be more gently frozen in bulk than in one's own freezer.

STORING VEGETABLES CORRECTLY

It goes without saying that vegetables should always be eaten when they are as fresh as possible, but often stocking up on vegetables cannot be avoided. Almost all vegetables can be stored in the vegetable compartment of the refrigerator, loosely packed and at the correct temperature. However, each vegetable type has its own individual storage time (see THE A-Z OF VEGETABLES). Vegetables can be stored for several months at -18°C /0.4°F in a freezer compartment or chest freezer. It is important only to freeze fresh, undamaged, blanched vegetables. Some types of vegetable should be cooked before freezing, for example aubergines, chicory and some types of bean.

Storage times vary from 3 months (aubergines) to 10 months (types of cabbage, pulses).

Industrially frozen vegetables provide another storage possibility, where small portions can be sold. Prepared frozen vegetables can be stored for several weeks in a home freezer compartment or chest freezer. When buying these products, make sure that the packaging is not damaged. The time which elapses between buying them and putting them back into storage should be short, so that the vegetables do not thaw. Thawed or defrosted vegetables must be used immediately.

Yet another way of storing vegetables is to bottle or pickle them in liquid made from vinegar, salt, sugar and spices. Vinegar prevents the development of mould and putrifying or fermenting bacteria. The correct mixture of vinegar and other ingredients gives vegetables a spicy, sweet-and-sour flavour. Pickled vegetables go well with meat dishes.

TRIMMING, WASHING AND CHOPPING VEGETABLES

Before cooking, vegetables have to be trimmed, washed and cut into slices or diced. Whether to peel or not is largely a matter of personal taste, but in the interests of healthy eating one should remember that a lot of vitamins and minerals are concentrated in the skin. Onions and garlic are always peeled. Trimmed vegetables should never be washed after chopping or slicing, to prevent water-soluble vitamins and minerals from leaching out. If chopped vegetables are not to be used immediately, they should be covered with a damp cloth. This protects the vegetables from reacting with oxygen (oxidation), which often turns vegetables brown. Sprinkling vegetables with lemon juice or vinegar also prevents this discolouration.

VEGETABLE CALENDAR

The months shown on the calendar indicate the main harvesting period. Almost all types are available as imports and from greenhouses outside these months.

Vegetable	J	F	M	A	M	J	J	A	S	O	N	D
Artichoke						▬	▬	▬	▬	▬		
Asparagus				▬	▬	▬						
Aubergine							▬	▬	▬	▬		
Broccoli						▬	▬	▬	▬	▬	▬	
Brussels sprouts	▬	▬	▬									
Carrots						▬	▬	▬	▬	▬	▬	▬
Cauliflower						▬	▬	▬	▬	▬		
Celeriac								▬	▬	▬	▬	▬
Celery						▬	▬	▬	▬	▬	▬	
Chicory									▬	▬	▬	▬
Common cabbage	▬											
Corn on the cob								▬	▬	▬		
Courgettes						▬	▬	▬	▬			
Cucumber						▬	▬	▬	▬	▬		
Fennel						▬	▬	▬	▬	▬		
Green beans						▬	▬	▬	▬	▬		
Kohlrabi					▬	▬	▬	▬	▬	▬		
Leeks								▬	▬	▬	▬	▬
Onions	▬	▬	▬				▬	▬	▬	▬	▬	▬
Peas						▬	▬	▬				
Peppers								▬	▬	▬		
Red cabbage	▬								▬	▬	▬	▬
Savoy cabbage	▬						▬	▬	▬	▬	▬	▬
Scorzonera	▬	▬	▬							▬	▬	▬
Spinach				▬	▬	▬	▬	▬	▬	▬		
Swiss Chard								▬	▬	▬		
Tomatoes						▬	▬	▬	▬	▬		
Turnips	▬	▬	▬			▬	▬	▬	▬	▬		
White cabbage	▬	▬	▬	▬	▬	▬	▬	▬	▬	▬	▬	▬

COOKING VEGETABLES

Regardless of how vegetables are cooked, the process should be quick so that the vegetables stay firm, with as little vitamins lost in the water as possible.

It is not necessary to arrange the following cooking methods per type of vegetable, since in general all vegetables can be cooked in any of these ways. Green beans, for example, can be blanched, boiled, steamed or braised.

Blanching means boiling vegetables in water and then cooling them in cold water. To prevent the vitamins leaching out excessively, a little salt should be added to the water. If vinegar or lemon juice is added to the water the vegetables will retain more colour.

Blanching makes vegetables more pleasurable to eat or work with, particularly spinach and some types of cabbage. It takes the bitterness out of chicory, prepares vegetables for freezing, makes the skin easier to remove (tomatoes, for example) and makes leaf vegetables easier to shape.

Blanching times vary between a few seconds for delicate vegetables (young spinach, tomatoes) and 2-4 minutes for more sturdy types (cabbage). Except for spinach, the blanching water should be saved because it contains many nutrients and can be used in sauces and soups.

Steaming without pressure is a fat-free, extremely gentle cooking method, which involves cooking the vegetables in water vapour. The vegetables do not come into contact with water. All you need is a saucepan with

Fresh vegetables in great variety are available all year round.

a tightly fitting lid and a steamer. Cover the base of the saucepan with about 4cm/1½ inches of water. Season and bring to the boil. Then place the vegetables in the steamer over the saucepan and steam gently, depending on type. Using this method, many vegetables take between 15 and 20 minutes to cook.

Steaming with pressure has its advantages and disadvantages. Although the shorter cooking time does retain the nutrients better, the flavours cannot develop properly during this time. The vegetables therefore have less flavour than when cooked without pressure. A pressure-cooker should only be used when time is genuinely of the essence. The cooking times given in recipes must be observed carefully to prevent over-cooking the vegetables.

Sweating is another gentle way of cooking vegetables. This involves cooking chopped or sliced vegetables with a little fat and/or liquid, at just below boiling point. Use a large frying-pan so that the vegetables can lie flat next to each other. First heat the fat, then add the vegetables and seasoning,

including salt, cover and sweat for 1-2 minutes. This allows the typical smells and flavours of the vegetables to develop. Only then should a little water be added and the vegetables cooked over a low heat until firm. When the cooking process is complete only a little liquid should be left. Cooking times may be a little longer than for steaming without pressure.

Glazing is a version of sweating. As well as fat and/or liquid, sugar is also added to the saucepan, so that the vegetables are given a shiny coating. It is important to remove the lid when two-thirds of the cooking time has elapsed so that most of the liquid can evaporate. In addition, the vegetables should be tossed frequently during cooking. Pearl onions, turnips, carrots and chestnuts are especially suitable for cooking in this way.

Boiling means cooking in bubbling, slightly salted liquid in a fully covered saucepan. This cooking method causes the most leaching from vegetables which is why it is best for cooking whole vegetables, such as cauliflower. There should be sufficient water in the saucepan just to cover the

vegetables. In addition, the vegetables should be placed straight into the vigorously boiling water, then cooked until firm in water which is just boiling gently.

Braising is usually only used for stuffed vegetable dishes (such as for aubergines, cucumber, courgettes and cabbage). The stuffed vegetable should be placed on a bed of finely chopped vegetables, such as carrot slices and onion rings. First, brown all the vegetables and then just cover in liquid (vegetable stock) and cook in the oven. Braising juices from which the fat has been skimmed make a good base for vegetable stock.

Frying is good for sliced vegetables such as aubergines, courgettes, artichoke hearts, potatoes and mushrooms. Season the vegetable slices and fry them in oil or butter. Place on absorbent paper after frying to remove excess fat.

COOKING FROZEN VEGETABLES

Frozen vegetables can be sweated or boiled. To sweat, place a little butter, the frozen vegetables, a little liquid and seasoning in a saucepan. Cover and sweat. To boil, place the frozen vegetables in vigorously boiling salted water and cook, covered. Cooking times for frozen vegetables are much shorter than for fresh vegetables because they have been blanched before freezing and because the cell structure of the vegetables loosens with freezing.

COOKING WHOLE ARTICHOKES

1. Always break off the stalk right next to the base so that the fibres in the heart come away with the stalk.
2. Cut about 3-4cm/1½-2 inches from the leaf tips using a carving knife.
3. Remove the small lower leaves and cut away the remaining leaves from the base using a sharp knife.
4. Remove the tips from the remaining leaves using scissors. If the prepared artichoke is not to be cooked immediately, soak it in slightly salted, acidulated water.
5. Put the artichoke in salted, boiling water to which a few drops of lemon juice have been added, cover and simmer for 20 minutes.
6. Twist out the inner leaves; set aside.
7. Using a sharp spoon, scoop out the choke from the heart. Replace the inner leaves, upside-down.

3.

4.

5.

COOKING ARTICHOKE HEARTS

1. Pull off the stalk right next to the base so that the fibres come away with the stalk. Remove the outer leaves by hand.
2. Carefully cut off the medium-sized leaves immediately above the base, using a large sharp knife.
3. Now carefully remove any remaining leaves from the base, using a small sharp knife.
4. Using a sharp spoon, remove all the inedible choke.
5. Either rub the prepared artichoke heart with lemon or place in slightly salted acidulated water before boiling, so that it does not discolour.
6. Boil the hearts in salted water to which a few drops of lemon juice have been added until just tender.

3.

4.

5.

1.

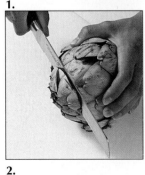

2.

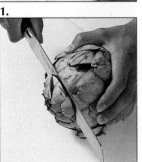

6.

7.

1.

2.

6.

Artichoke heart

STUFFING AUBERGINES

1. Halve the aubergines lengthways. Make several criss-cross incisions in the flesh, using a sharp knife.

2. Place the halves, with the cut surfaces face down, on a lightly oiled baking sheet and brown in the oven.

3. When the aubergine flesh is soft, remove it using a sharp spoon or a melon baller.

4. Mix the chopped flesh with 250g/8oz minced raw meat, a finely diced red pepper, 3 tablespoons of cooked rice and 2 crushed garlic cloves. Season with salt, pepper and paprika and use the mixture to fill the aubergine halves.

5. Place the stuffed aubergines in a buttered ovenproof dish. Cover with sliced tomato, sprinkle with grated cheese and drizzle with oil.

6. Cook in the oven until browned.

3.

4.

5.

STUFFING CUCUMBERS

1. Thinly peel the cucumbers, removing each end.

2. Cut the cucumbers in half crossways. Using a thin wooden spoon handle, loosen the core, then carefully push it out using a thicker handle.

3. For the stuffing, mix together 200g/7oz minced raw meat, 4 tablespoons of finely diced red and green pepper and 1 tablespoon of chopped dill.

4. Put the stuffing into a piping bag fitted with a large nozzle and pipe into the cucumbers.

5. Butter a flat, ovenproof dish and cover the base with slices of carrot and onion. Place the cucumbers on top.

6. Season the cucumbers with salt, pepper and a pinch of sugar. Just cover with stock and cover the container with a lid or with aluminium foil.

7. Bring to the boil, then cook in a moderate oven for about 25 minutes.

3.

4.

5.

1.

1.

2.

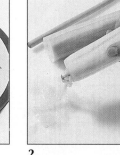

Stuffed aubergine

6.

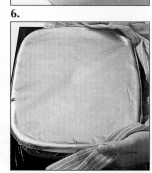

2.

7.

SLICING ONIONS

CHOPPING ONIONS

PREPARING TOMATOES

1. Cut the onion in half lengthways, then cut off the root end and the tip.

1. Halve the onions lengthways and make a vertical cut to just above the root.

1. Remove the stalks. Using a small sharp knife, make a shallow crossed incision in the base of each tomato.

4. To remove the seeds, halve the tomato and scoop them out with a small sharp spoon, without damaging the outer wall of the fruit.

2. Cut the prepared onion lengthways into slices.

2. Make several fine horizontal incisions in each onion half.

2. Briefly plunge into boiling water or pour boiling water over the tomatoes.

5. For salads, wash thoroughly, cut out the stalk end by making a cone-shaped incision in the fruit, and cut into thin slices using a very sharp knife.

3. For onion rings, first cut the tip from the whole onion. Then cut the onion across into thin, even slices.

3. Finally, hold the onion firmly and slice thinly; it will fall into fine dice.

3. Cool immediately in cold water, peel and at the same time cut out the flower end, which contains solanine, and any green parts.

COOKING ASPARAGUS

1. If using white asparagus, peel before cooking. Peel the stalk from tip to base using a swivel-action vegetable peeler.
2. Wash the asparagus and divide into bundles. Loosely tie each portion together with kitchen string, so that the tips are all at the same level.
3. Trim the base of the asparagus spears to the same length.
4. Add 1 tablespoon of salt and 1 teaspoon of sugar to 1 litre/1¾ pints of water. Cook the asparagus in the water for about 15-18 minutes.

2.

3.

BLANCHING BROCCOLI

1. Remove any leaves from the broccoli. Divide the head into florets and wash them under cold running water.
2. Peel any large coarse stalks and cut them into slices.
3. To blanch, put the broccoli florets and the stalks into boiling, salted water for 2-3 minutes.
4. Remove the broccoli from the boiling water and cool in cold water (do not use ice).
5. Place the broccoli in a colander to drain.

3.

4.

1.

4.

1.

5.

Boiled white asparagus

2.

Broccoli ready to serve

Hearty Home Cooking

*T*here was a time when no courgettes, aubergines, peppers, fennel or okra were available to us. Vegetable dishes consisted of cabbage and sprouts, beans and leeks, turnips – and of course potatoes, potatoes and more potatoes! But housewives really knew how to transform them into tasty everyday meals and feasts for special occasions! We still like broad beans, stuffed cabbage, potato pancakes and Brussels sprouts. So in this chapter we have brought together the best vegetable recipes using the kind of vegetables that used to be available in abundance from every kitchen garden. If some of the quantities seem large (as in the broad bean recipe on page 36) or the vegetables hard to find (as with fresh grated horseradish on page 39) this is because we know that people like to grow these traditional crops in their own gardens or on their allotments.

Beetroot with Bacon
(see recipe on page 39)

MUSHROOMS IN CREAM SAUCE

SERVES 4 ■
*Preparation and cooking
time: 30 minutes
Kcal per portion: 450
P = 9g, F = 41g, C = 6g*

1kg/2¼lbs button mushrooms
2 shallots
100g/4oz butter
juice of ½ lemon
250ml/8 fl oz single cream
salt and pepper
2 tbsps brandy
1 tbsp chopped chervil

*Cut off the stalk ends, then wipe
the mushrooms.*

1. Cut off the stalks (use
these in soup) and wipe the
mushrooms with absorbent
paper. Slice the mushrooms
evenly. Finely chop the shallots.
2. Heat the butter in a large
frying-pan and sweat the
shallots until transparent.
Add the mushrooms and
continue cooking until all
the liquid has evaporated
and the mushrooms begin to
change colour. Pour in the
lemon juice.

*Braise the thinly sliced
mushrooms in butter with the
diced shallots.*

3. Put the cream in a small
saucepan and bring to the
boil. Add almost all of it to
the mushrooms and cook
over medium heat until
reduced. Season with salt
and pepper to taste.
4. Combine the brandy with
the remaining cream and
pour over the mushrooms.
Bring back to the boil , then
remove from the heat. Serve
immediately, sprinkled with
chervil.

*Heat most of the cream, pour
over the vegetables and reduce.*

Accompaniment: new potatoes; or arrange on four
slices of toast and serve as a
starter.

BROAD BEANS

SERVES 4 ■
*Preparation and cooking
time: 1 hour
Kcal per portion: 1425
P = 88g, F = 37g, C = 184g*

2.5kg/5lbs 6oz fresh broad
  beans
150g/5½oz smoked rindless
  bacon
20 spring onions (white parts
  only)
1 large onion
1 bunch parsley
1 tbsp oil
475ml/15 fl oz vegetable stock
1 tsp dried savory
salt and pepper
2 tbsps crème fraîche

1. Remove the beans from
their pods and wash them.
Finely dice the bacon.
2. Wash and trim the spring
onions. Finely chop the
onion and parsley.
3. Melt the oil in a casserole
and sweat the bacon until
the fat is transparent. Add
the onion and parsley
(reserve some parsley for
garnishing) and sweat
briefly. Add the beans and
fry for a few minutes.
4. Pour the stock over the
vegetables. Add the savory,
salt and pepper. Cook the
beans over a medium heat
for about 40 minutes.
5. 10 minutes before the end
of the cooking time, remove
the lid so that the liquid can
reduce completely.
6. Add the crème fraîche to
the vegetables and bring to
the boil. Serve sprinkled with
the reserved parsley.
Accompaniment: new potatoes.

KOHLRABI

SERVES 4 ■
*Preparation and cooking
time: 25 minutes
Kcal per portion: 115
P = 4g, F = 6g, C = 10g*

6 young kohlrabi
250ml/8 fl oz water
salt
30g/1oz butter
1 tbsp flour
freshly grated nutmeg

*First remove any green leaves
from the kohlrabi, then peel.
Reserve young tender leaves, chop
finely and add to the kohlrabi just
before the end of the cooking
time.*

1. Peel the kohlrabi and cut
into thin slices or match-
sticks. If there are any leaves,
wash them, roll up and cut
into strips.
2. Put the kohlrabi slices and
the water into a saucepan
with a little salt. Cook, covered, over a medium heat for
about 15 minutes. Add the
leaves just before the end of
the cooking time.
3. In the meantime, thoroughly mash together the
butter and flour with a fork
to make beurre manié. Stir
this into the kohlrabi in small
lumps to thicken the liquid
and bring to the boil. Season
with nutmeg to taste.
An accompaniment to fried
meat.

RED
CABBAGE

TASTY POTATO CAKES

SERVES 4 ■
Preparation and cooking time: 45 minutes
Kcal per portion: 240
P = 7g, F = 13g, C = 25g

500g/1lb2oz floury potatoes
salt
50g/2oz flour
2 eggs, separated
2 tbsps single cream
freshly grated nutmeg
oil and butter for frying

1. Peel and quarter the potatoes. Cook, just covered in salted water. Discard the boiling water and shake the potatoes in the saucepan until completely dry.
2. Press the potatoes through a potato ricer or vegetable mill into a bowl. Add the flour, egg yolks,

> ### TIP
> *For a change, add finely chopped herbs or finely diced onion, fried in butter until transparent, to the potato dough.*

cream, salt to taste and nutmeg. Beat the egg whites until stiff and fold into the mixture.
3. Heat 1 tablespoon of oil and 15g/½oz butter in a large frying-pan. Using a spoon, place small balls of potato dough in the pan and press flat. Fry until pale brown, turn carefully and fry the other side until golden.
An accompaniment to meat and game dishes, or vegetable dishes without meat, e.g. served with French beans as a main meal.

Press the boiled potatoes through a potato ricer.

Fold the beaten egg white into the seasoned potato mixture.

Fry the potato cakes on both sides until golden.

CREAMED POTATO WITH CRESS

SERVES 4 ■
Preparation and cooking time: 30 minutes
Kcal per portion: 240
P = 6g, F = 9g, C = 34

1kg/2¼lbs floury potatoes
salt
250ml/8 fl oz milk
30g/1oz butter
1 carton mustard and cress
freshly grated nutmeg

1. Peel and finely dice the potatoes. Place in a saucepan, just covered with water. Add salt and boil for 15 minutes until soft. Pour away the water. Dry the potatoes by shaking the saucepan.
2. Heat the milk in a large saucepan. Press the potatoes through a potato ricer

> ### TIP
> *Instead of cress, chopped herbs such as parsley or dill, or finely grated raw carrot can be added to the creamed potato.*

or vegetable mill into the milk. Whisk until the mixture is creamy.
3. Season with salt to taste, then stir in the butter in small knobs. Finely chop the mustard and cress with scissors and add to the creamed potato. Season with nutmeg. An accompaniment to baked fish or meat.

CREAMED POTATO AU GRATIN

SERVES 4 ■■
Preparation and cooking time: 50 minutes
Kcal per portion: 685
P = 35g, F = 45g, C = 34g

1kg/2¼lbs floury potatoes
salt
250ml/8 fl oz milk
60g/2oz butter
freshly grated nutmeg
3 eggs, beaten
2 tbsps creamed horseradish
300g/10oz Cheddar cheese

1. Peel and finely dice the potatoes. Put into a saucepan, just cover with water, add salt and boil for 15 minutes until soft.
2. Pour away the water. Keep the saucepan over the heat and shake until the potatoes are completely dry.
3. Heat the milk in a large saucepan. Press the diced potato through a potato ricer or vegetable mill into the hot milk. Whisk until the mixture becomes creamy. Stir in the butter in small knobs. Season with salt and nutmeg.
4. Add the eggs, horseradish and 250g/8oz of cheese to the creamed potato.
5. Butter a baking dish. Heat the oven to 200°C/400°F/Gas Mark 6.
6. Transfer the potato mixture into a piping bag. Pipe the mixture into the baking dish. Sprinkle with the remaining cheese.
7. Bake in the centre of the oven for 20 minutes, until golden.
An accompaniment to fried fish or meat dishes; can also be served with salad as a vegetarian meal.

Dishes from Around the World

*O*ur foreign neighbours – both close at hand and further afield – have always known how to prepare vegetables, particularly in countries around the Mediterranean and in the Orient. The selection of wonderful vegetables always available cheaply in the markets inspired culinary imagination and produced a wealth of recipes. Even in our own country, aubergines, courgettes, artichokes, avocados and chicory are no longer just occasional guests. We can now choose all year round from an enormous range of vegetables and make dishes that bring aromas and flavours from all over the world into our kitchens.

Savoy Cabbage Indian Style
(see recipe on page 52)

VALAIS-STYLE CHARD ROLLS

SERVES 4   ■ ■
*Preparation and cooking
time: 1½ hours
Kcal per portion: 920
P = 32g, F = 75g, C = 30g*

*24 large chard leaves
2 tbsps oil
600ml/18 fl oz milk
300ml/12 fl oz stock
½ Continental pork sausage
100g/4oz grated cheese
45g/1½oz butter*

FOR THE FILLING:
*150g/5½oz wholemeal flour
2 eggs
salt and pepper
freshly grated nutmeg
100ml/3 fl oz water
50g/2oz rindless streaky
    bacon
30g/1oz cooked ham
100g/4oz onion, finely diced
3 small smoked sausages
1 kabanos sausage (200g/7oz)
1 bunch parsley
45g/1½oz chard leaves
1 sprig thyme
1 sprig rosemary
½ bunch chives
30g/1oz butter*

1. First prepare the filling. Put the flour into a bowl. Make a well in the centre and put in the eggs, salt, pepper and nutmeg. Using a fork, mix the eggs with some of the flour.
2. Add the water, stirring with a wooden spoon. Continue beating until the mixture becomes smooth and creamy. Leave to stand for 30 minutes.
3. Meanwhile finely dice the bacon, ham and sausages. finely chop the parsley, chard leaves and remaining herbs.
4. Melt the butter in a frying-pan and brown the diced meat and onion. Add the herbs and stir briefly. Thoroughly mix this mixture, while hot, into the egg and flour mixture. Cool.

5. Wash the chard leaves and blanch in salted water. Drain well and spread out on a board. Place 1 tablespoon of filling on each leaf. Fold the sides of the leaves over the filling and roll up lengthways.
6. Heat the oil in a frying-pan and carefully brown the rolls all over.
7. Heat the oven to 220°C/425°F/Gas Mark 7.
8. Bring the milk and stock to the boil in a flameproof dish. Place the rolls side by side in the liquid and simmer for 15 minutes over a low heat.
9. Skin and chop the pork sausage and sprinkle over the chard rolls. Top with the cheese and dot with butter. Brown in the centre of the oven until the cheese melts. If you cannot obtain chard leaves, large spinach beet leaves will do.
Accompaniment: noodles or rice.
Recommended drink: strong, young red wine from Valais

The filling for the rolls is made from a seasoned dough of eggs and flour, flavoured with chopped herbs, onions, ham, bacon and chard leaves.

Place 1 tablespoon of the cooled filing mixture on each leaf.

Place the spinach beet rolls in the milk and stock mixture. Sprinkle with chopped pork sausage and grated cheese. Dot with butter and bake.

BAKED POTATOES WITH CREAMY ROQUEFORT

SERVES 4   ■
*Preparation and cooking
time: 1 hour
Kcal per portion: 540
P = 14g, F = 38g, C = 34g*

*8 baking potatoes
2 ripe avocados
4 tbsps crème fraîche
100g/4 oz quark or curd
    cheese
60g/2oz Roquefort cheese
juice of ½ lemon
45g/1½oz red caviar*

1. Heat the oven to 220°C/425°F/Gas Mark 7.
2. Wash the potatoes and dry with absorbent paper. Put each one on a square piece of aluminium foil. Fold the corners upward and squeeze together to enclose the potatoes.
3. Place the parcels directly on a shelf in the centre of the oven for 50-60 minutes or until cooked.
4. Meanwhile halve the avocados lengthways, stone and peel. Chop the flesh and purée in a liquidiser.
5. Mix the crème Fraîche with the quark or curd cheese. Mash the Roquefort with a fork and stir into the quark mixture. Stir the avocado purée into the mixture and season with the lemon juice.
6. Take the cooked potatoes out of the oven and remove the Foil. Cut a cross in each potato and open out slightly. Divide the Roquefort cream between the potatoes and garnish with the caviar.
Accompaniment: mixed salad.
Recommended drink: crisp, dry white wine, e.g. Chablis.

SERBIAN-STYLE PEPPERS

SERVES 4 ■

Preparation and cooking time: 30 minutes
Kcal per portion: 335
P = 6g, F = 29g, C = 13g

1kg/2¼lbs yellow peppers
750g/1½lbs tomatoes
50g/2oz rindless smoked bacon
90g/3½oz pork dripping or lard
2 large onions
1 tbsp paprika
salt

1. Halve, core, de-seed and wash the peppers. Slice into strips. Blanch the tomatoes in boiling water. Peel and quarter.
2. Dice the bacon. Heat the fat in a frying-pan and sweat

> **TIP**
>
> *A complete main course dish can be made by adding slices of smoked dried sausage to the peppers.*

the bacon until the fat is transparent. Dice the onion, add to the pan and brown.
3. Add the strips of pepper and tomato quarters to the frying-pan. Sprinkle with paprika and fry the vegetables over a low heat for 20 minutes, stirring from time to time. Season with salt to taste.
Accompaniment: rice or un-peeled boiled potatoes.
Recommended drink: red vin de pays.

HUNGARIAN STUFFED PEPPERS

SERVES 4 ■ ■

Preparation and cooking time: 1¾ hours
Kcal per portion: 465
P = 33g, F = 23g, C = 31g

8 large green peppers
100g/4oz rice
salt and pepper
500g/1lb2oz boneless lamb
2 small onions
1 garlic clove
1 tbsp finely chopped mint
1 tbsp finely chopped dill
250ml/8 fl oz stock
15g/½oz butter
150g/5½oz crème fraîche

1. Cut small lids from the peppers. Carefully remove the cores and seeds and wash the inside and outside of the peppers.
2. Pre-cook the rice in a little salted water for 5 minutes. Drain in a sieve.

> **TIP**
>
> *Tomato sauce, made from fresh tomatoes, can be poured over the peppers instead of crème fraîche.*

3. Put the meat, onion and garlic through a mincer or chop, not too finely, in a food processor. Mix with the rice and herbs. Season well with salt and pepper. Stuff the peppers with the meat. Place upright in an oven-proof dish and cover with the lids removed earlier.
4. Heat the oven to 200°C/400°F/Gas Mark 6.
5. Heat the butter and stock in a saucepan until the butter has melted. Pour over the peppers. Cover the dish with a lid or foil.

Chop the meat, onions and garlic in a food processor. Mix with the rice and herbs, and season.

Put the lids back on the stuffed peppers. Place the peppers upright in an ovenproof dish or pan, close together so that they cannot fall over. Pour over the butter and stock and bake in the oven.

6. Cook the peppers on the bottom shelf of the oven For 60-70 minutes. Place on a serving plate and keep warm. Stir the crème fraîche into the pan juices and cook until reduced to a creamy sauce. Serve with the peppers.
Accompaniment: rice.
Recommended drink: full-bodied, aromatic red wine.

MORELS WITH CREAM

SERVES 4 ■

Preparation and cooking time: 45 minutes
Soaking time for dried morels: 1 hour
Kcal per portion: 365
P = 4g, F = 33g, C = 10g

500g/1lb2oz fresh or 50g/2oz dried morels
60g/2oz butter
salt and pepper
juice of ½ lemon
200g/7oz crème fraîche
2 tbsps brandy

1. Soak dried morels For 1 hour; place fresh morels in cold water for 5 minutes. Wash the mushrooms thoroughly under running water to remove sand from under the wrinkled cap.
2. Halve or quarter large mushrooms. Dry carefully with absorbent paper. Pour the soaking water from dried morels through a fine sieve into a bowl.
3. Melt the butter in a flame-proof casserole. Add the mushrooms and season with salt, pepper and lemon juice. Cook for 10 minutes over a low heat, stirring from time to time.
4. Add a little cream and, if using dried morels, the soaking water. Cook for a few minutes to reduce the liquid.
5. Add the brandy and the remaining cream. Simmer to make a thick creamy sauce. An accompaniment to fillet steak, veal cutlets or lamb chops (use half quantities). Can also be used as a vol-au-vent filling.

MOUSSAKA

SERVES 4 ■■

*Preparation and cooking
time: 2 hours
Kcal per portion: 605
P = 36g, F = 45g, C = 14g*

6 aubergines (about
    1kg/2¼lbs)
salt and pepper
flour
125ml/4 fl oz olive oil
500g/1lb2oz minced lamb
2 small onions
500g/1lb2oz tomatoes
200g/7oz yoghurt
3 eggs
butter for the dish

1. Cut the aubergines into thin slices lengthways. Sprinkle salt over the cut surfaces and leave for 30 minutes to draw out the bitter juice.

2. Pour away the juice and wash the slices. Dry them on absorbent paper and toss in flour. Heat half the olive oil in a large frying-pan and fry the aubergine slices in batches until pale brown.

3. Break up the minced lamb and dice the onions. Heat the remaining oil. First brown the meat, then add the diced onion and fry until transparent. Season with salt and pepper.

4. Blanch the tomatoes in boiling water. Peel and slice thinly.

5. Heat the oven to 200°C/400°F/Gas Mark 6.

6. Butter a baking dish and cover the base with a third of the aubergine slices. Cover with sliced tomato and half the minced meat mixture. Then add another layer of aubergines, tomatoes, minced meat and the remaining aubergine slices. Bake in the centre of the oven for about 30 minutes.

7. Mix together the yoghurt, eggs, 1 tablespoon of flour and salt and pour over the aubergines. Bake for a further 15 minutes, until the crust is golden brown.

While the salted aubergine slices are soaking, brown the minced meat in hot oil, add the diced onion and fry until transparent.

Arrange two layers each of aubergines, tomatoes and minced meat in a baking dish. Before browning, pour over the yoghurt and egg sauce.

Recommended drink:
full-bodied red wine, such as a Corbières, Côtes de Provence or Chianti.

RATATOUILLE

SERVES 10 ■■■

*Preparation and cooking
time: 3 hours
Kcal per portion: 575
P = 6g, F = 51g, C = 18g*

3 large Spanish onions
3 garlic cloves
250ml/8 fl oz olive oil
1kg/2¼lbs beefsteak tomatoes
125ml/4 fl oz tomato juice
125ml/4 fl oz dry white wine
1 bouquet garni (2 bay
    leaves, rosemary and
    thyme sprigs, 3 parsley
    sprigs)
salt and pepper
2 red and 2 yellow peppers
    (about 750g/1½lbs)
1.5kg/3lbs 6oz aubergines
1.5kg/3lbs 6oz courgettes

1. Slice the onions and crush the garlic cloves with the back of a knife. Blanch the tomatoes in boiling water. Peel and chop, removing the hard yellow cores.

2. Heat 4 tbsps of the oil in a large heavy pan. Fry the onions until transparent, then add the tomatoes and garlic cloves. Pour in the tomato juice and half the white wine. Add the bouquet garni, salt and pepper and stew over a low heat for 10 minutes.

3. Meanwhile halve, core and de-seed the peppers. Slice into strips.

4. Wash the aubergines and courgettes, then slice thickly. Heat another 4 tbsps of oil in a saucepan. Cook these vegetables over a high heat, stirring from time to time, until golden.

5. Heat the oven to 190°C/375°F/Gas Mark 5.

6. Heat the remaining oil in another saucepan and brown the sliced peppers.

7. Put all the vegetables in the saucepan with the onion and tomato mixture. Add the remaining wine and cover the pan.

8. Place in the centre of the oven and stew for 2 hours.

Remove the vegetables using a slotted spoon. Drain briefly (the vegetables should still be soaked in olive oil) and place in a serving dish.

This dish tastes even better the following day, whether served hot or cold.

Accompaniment:
fresh French bread.

Recommended drink:
red vin de pays or a light French rosé.

> **TIP**
>
> *Preparing this ratatouille is really only worthwhile if you are catering for a large group of people. Since each vegetable must be pre-cooked individually, it takes a lot of time and effort. Ensure that you have a big enough pot to hold the entire mixture.*

GRATIN DAUPHINOIS

SERVES 4 ■
*Preparation and cooking
time: 1 hour
Kcal per portion: 430
P = 10g, F = 28g, C = 34g*

*1kg/2¼lbs floury potatoes
250ml/8 fl oz single cream
1 garlic clove
60g/2oz butter
salt and pepper
freshly grated nutmeg
50g/2oz Gruyère cheese*

1. Peel and wash the potatoes. Slice very thinly (preferably in a food processor). Put the slices into cold water for a couple of minutes, then drain in a sieve and dry with absorbent paper.
2. Bring the cream to the boil in a small saucepan. Cut the garlic clove in half and rub the inside of a large shallow baking dish with the cut surfaces. Grease with a third of the butter.
3. Heat the oven to 200°C/400°F/Gas Mark 6.
4. Arrange a third of the sliced potato in the dish and season generously with salt,

> ### TIP
> *If you are serving the gratin with a particularly tender meat dish, omit the cheese so that it does not overpower its delicate flavour.*

pepper and nutmeg. Grate the cheese and sprinkle half over the potato. Arrange half the remaining potatoes on top, season again and sprinkle with the remaining cheese.
5. Make a third layer from the remaining potato, arranging them carefully. Season with salt and pepper and pour over the cream.

Thinly slice the potatoes in a food processor.

Arrange potatoes, seasoning and cheese in alternate layers in an ovenproof dish. Pour the cream over the top.

6. Dot the remaining butter over the gratin. Bake the potatoes on the bottom shelf of the oven for 45 minutes until golden. Test to see if the potatoes are done. If not cook for a little longer.
An accompaniment to grilled and roast lamb or other meat dishes. Can also be served as a main dish with vegetables or a colourful, mixed salad.

SAVOY CABBAGE INDIAN STYLE

(see photo on page 44)

SERVES 4 ■
*Preparation and cooking
time: 30 minutes
Kcal per portion: 170
P = 7g, F = 12g, C = 9g*

*1 Savoy cabbage (about
    1kg/2¼lbs)
2-3 dried red chillies
salt
3 tbsps oil
1 tsp mustard seeds
1 tbsp chick-pea flour
2 tbsps finely chopped fresh
    ginger root
1 tsp turmeric
3 tbsps desiccated coconut*

1. Pull any limp leaves from the cabbage. Separate the remaining leaves, wash and slice into fine strips. Wash, halve, de-seed and finely chop the chillies.
2. Bring a little salted water to the boil in a saucepan. Blanch the strips of cabbage quickly in the water, then drain in a sieve.
3. Heat the oil in a deep non-stick frying-pan and fry the mustard seeds briefly. Add the chick-pea flour, chillies, ginger, turmeric, coconut and cabbage.
4. Fry vigorously over a high heat for a few minutes. Then cook over a low heat for 10 minutes until soft, stirring occasionally. Season with salt.
Accompaniment:
boiled brown rice.
Recommended drink:
mineral water or beer.

COURGETTE OMELETTES

SERVES 4 ■
*Preparation and cooking
time: 40 minutes
Kcal per portion: 475
P = 27g, F = 33g, C = 19g*

*6 small courgettes (about
    750g/1½lbs)
1 tsp salt
4 eggs
4 garlic cloves
1 bunch parsley
200g/7oz mature Cheddar
    cheese
6-8 tbsps self-raising flour
oil for frying*

1. Wash and trim the courgettes; grate coarsely. Put into a bowl and stir in the salt and eggs.
2. Finely chop the garlic cloves and parsley and grate the cheese. Add to the courgette mixture and sift in enough flour to make a firm dough. Mix together thoroughly.

> ### TIP
> *These delicate courgette omelettes with cheese make a satisfying vegetarian main dish.*

3. Heat a generous amount of oil in a large frying-pan. Using a spoon, put small balls of courgette dough into the oil and press flat. Fry on both sides until brown and crispy. Serve immediately.
Accompaniment:
tomato salad or mixed salad.
Serves 6-8 as a side dish.
Recommended drink:
crisp, white vin de pays.

Cooking for Special Occasions

*V*egetables have become an established and highly regarded part of the cuisine for all discerning gourmets. Imagine the menu of a high-class restaurant without those melt-in-the-mouth vegetable flans and purées, cabbage with sparkling wine or vegetable strudel. Distinctive fillings elevate kohlrabi, mushrooms, courgettes and aubergines into delicacies. Delicately seasoned creamy sauces are compulsory with many dishes. A vegetable dish such as Stuffed Artichokes or Scorzonera Fritters can prove a worthy start to the most ambitious dinner. Vegetables offer a limitless range of possibilities, taking both leading and supporting roles in vegetarian meals for special occasions.

Sauerkraut with Sparkling Wine (see recipe on page 67)

BRUSSELS SPROUT RING WITH MUSHROOM AND NUT SAUCE

SERVES 4 ■■

Preparation and cooking time: 45-50 minutes
Kcal per portion: 395
P = 8g, F = 36g, C = 7g

250g/8oz Brussels sprouts
4 tbsps milk
6 tbsps cream
3 egg yolks
salt and pepper

FOR THE SAUCE:
45g/1½oz butter, softened
30g/1oz ground hazelnuts
100g/4oz mushrooms
2 shallots
3 tbsps dry white wine
100g/4oz single cream
100ml/3 fl oz vegetable stock
cayenne
chervil leaves to garnish

1. Start the sauce by making a paste from 30g/1oz of the butter and ground nuts. Fill a large bowl with ice cubes. Place the bowl containing the nut butter inside the larger bowl and put in the refrigerator.
2. Heat the oven to 200°C/400°F/Gas Mark 6.
3. Trim the Brussels sprouts. Steam or boil in salted water until still firm. Cool immediately in ice-cold water. Drain and blend in a liquidiser, with the milk. Put the cream in a small saucepan and cook until reduced by half. Cool slightly, then mix with the egg yolks and stir into the Brussels sprout purée. Season with salt and pepper.
4. Butter a ring mould and fill it with the mixture. Stand in a baking tin half-full of hot water and cook in the oven for about 20-25 minutes.
5. Meanwhile make the sauce. Wipe the mushrooms and dice very finely, along with the shallots. Heat the

Fill a ring mould with the Brussels sprout purée. Place in a water bath and bake until firm.

remaining 15g/½oz butter and fry the mushrooms and shallots gently. Add the wine, boil briefly and pass through a sieve into a small saucepan. Add the cream and vegetable stock and cook until the sauce is light and creamy. Beat the ice-cold nut butter into the sauce. Season with salt, pepper and a pinch of cayenne.
6. Carefully turn out the ring onto a serving plate. Fill the centre with the mushrooms and nut sauce. Garnish with chervil leaves.
Serve as a starter.
Recommended drink: dry white wine.

> **TIP**
>
> *Broccoli or Savoy cabbage can be used instead of Brussels sprouts. The flan mixture can also be cooked in serving-sized moulds (soufflé dishes or ramekins). Before turning out, test the mixture with a cocktail stick to make sure it is firm.*

TOMATO-STUFFED COURGETTES

SERVES 4 ■■

Preparation and cooking time: 1 hour
Kcal per portion: 275
P = 6g, F = 23g, C = 10g

250g/8oz can tomatoes
4 medium courgettes
250g/8oz onions
3 garlic cloves
2 tbsps olive oil
1 tbsp chopped fresh rosemary
1 tbsp chopped fresh thyme
1 bay leaf
salt and pepper
50g/2oz black olives
1 egg
6 tbsps cream
butter for the dish

1. Wash the courgettes. Halve lengthways and hollow out using a teaspoon. Chop the flesh finely.
2. Drain the tomatoes and chop finely. Also chop the onions and garlic finely. Heat the olive oil in a saucepan, add all the vegetables, the rosemary, thyme and bay leaf and simmer for 20 minutes. Season to taste and cool.
3. Heat the oven to 180°C/350°F/Gas Mark 4.
4. Chop the olives and beat the egg with the cream. Stir into the vegetables and stuff the courgettes with this mixture. Butter a shallow baking dish, put in the stuffed courgettes and bake for about 30 minutes.
Accompaniment: crusty brown bread.
Recommended drink: Chianti.

SHALLOTS IN MUSHROOM AND CREAM SAUCE

SERVES 6-8 ■■

Preparation and cooking time: 55-60 minutes
Kcal per portion (8 portions): 105
P = 3g, F = 7g, C = 7g

750g/1½lbs shallots
300g/10z button mushrooms
15g/½oz butter
salt and white pepper
2 tbsps dry sherry
125ml/5 fl oz single cream
1 tbsp finely chopped chives

1. Blanch the shallots in boiling water for 2 minutes. Cool in cold water and peel. Place

> **TIP**
>
> *Shallots are particularly popular in French cuisine. They are milder than onions and more suitable for making delicately favoured sauces.*

in cold salted water, bring back to the boil and simmer for about 5 minutes.
2. Meanwhile wipe the mushrooms and heat the butter in a saucepan. Fry the mushrooms whole, tossing to cook them evenly.
3. Drain the shallots into a small saucepan. Heat the liquid until reduced to about 6 tablespoons. Add the shallots to the mushrooms.
4. Add the sherry and shallot liquid to the vegetables and cook until completely reduced. Add the cream and continue cooking until the sauce is creamy. Season with salt and pepper. Turn into a bowl, sprinkle with chives and serve as a side dish.

STUFFED ARTICHOKES

SERVES 4 ■ ■ ■
Preparation and cooking time: 70 minutes
Kcal per portion: 410
P = 12g, F = 35g, C = 9g

4 large artichokes
½ lemon
salt and pepper
90g/3½oz butter
150g/5½oz smoked salmon
2 tbsps cream
½ tsp lemon pepper
4 tbsps dry white wine
1 tbsp finely chopped shallot
3 egg yolks
a little lemon juice

1. Cut off the top third of the artichoke and snap off the stem. Rub the cut surfaces and bases immediately with lemon.
2. Boil the artichokes in very lightly salted water for 30-40 minutes (depending on size). Remove with a slotted spoon and cool. Loosen the outer leaves; remove the soft inner leaves and discard the bristly choke.
3. Generously butter four small ovenproof dishes (use about 15g/½oz).
4. Finely chop the smoked salmon. Using the back of a spoon, squeeze the artichoke flesh out of the inner leaves and mix it with the salmon, cream and lemon pepper.
5. Put the wine, shallot and a pinch of pepper into a small saucepan. Boil until only about 1 teaspoon of liquid remains.
6. Put the egg yolks into a heatproof bowl set over a pan of gently simmering water. Press the reduced wine and shallot mixture through a sieve into the egg yolks. Add a small knob of butter and beat over a medium heat until the sauce is creamy and sticks to the whisk.

7. Remove the bowl from the heat. Stir in the remaining butter, in small knobs. From time to time, return the bowl very briefly to the hot

TIP

When buying artichokes, make sure that the heads are tightly closed and have no black spots. An artichoke should feel heavy for its size and should not look dry.

water so that the sauce does not cool and the butter melts completely. As soon as all the butter has been used up season the sauce with salt and lemon juice.
8. Place the prepared salmon mixture in the artichokes. Pour over the sauce and brown for 1-2 minutes under a hot grill. Serve as a starter.
Recommended drink:
white Bordeaux.

SPINACH-STUFFED MUSHROOMS

SERVES 4 ■ ■
Preparation and cooking time: 50 minutes
Kcal per portion: 210
P = 6g, F = 17g, C = 4g

25 open-cup mushrooms
30g/1oz butter
100g/4oz button mushrooms
100g/4oz young spinach
1 bunch parsley
2 shallots
1 tsp oregano
salt and pepper
125ml/5 fl oz single cream
1 egg
6 tbsps white wine

1. Clean the open-cup mushrooms; remove and reserve the stalks. Grease a large ovenproof dish with half the butter and arrange the mushrooms in it, gills upward.
2. Wipe the button mushrooms. Wash the spinach and the parsley.
3. Chop the button mushrooms, reserved stalks, spinach and parsley.
4. Heat the oven to 220°C/425°F/Gas Mark 7.
5. Put the remaining butter in a saucepan. Finely chop the shallots and sweat until transparent. Add the mushrooms, spinach, parsley, oregano, salt and pepper. Cook briefly, then remove from the heat.
6. Mix the egg with the cream and stir into the mixture. Spoon into the mushrooms.
7. Sprinkle with the wine and cover the dish with aluminium foil. Cook in the oven for about 20 minutes. Serve as a starter.
Recommended drink:
spicy Müller-Thurgau from Baden or the Palatinate.

Clean the mushrooms with a brush.

Carefully separate the stalks from the caps.

Place the mushrooms in a buttered ovenproof dish.

Using a teaspoon, fill the mushrooms with the spinach mixture.

SCORZONERA IN PUFF PASTRY

SERVES 6 ■ ■ ■

*Preparation and cooking
time: 1 hour 20 minutes
Kcal per portion: 500
P = 13g, F = 35g, C = 32g*

500g/1lb2oz frozen puff
  pastry, thawed
butter and flour for the tin
1kg/2¼lbs scorzonera
1 tbsp lemon juice
150g/5½oz cooked ham
150g/5½oz broccoli
salt and pepper
1 egg yolk
4 tbsps dry white wine
125g/5oz crème fraîche

1. Roll out about two-thirds of the pastry 3mm/⅛ inch

> ### TIP
> *Clean scorzonera with a brush under running water and peel using a swivel vegetable peeler. Always wear plastic or rubber gloves when peeling scorzonera, because the juice stains the skin.*

thick. Butter and flour a 23-cm/9 inch springform cake tin. Line with the pastry and put in the refrigerator.
2. Peel the scorzonera and place immediately in water containing a squeeze of lemon juice, to keep it white.
3. Dice the ham. Divide the broccoli into small florets. Heat the oven to 220°C/425°F/Gas Mark 7.
4. Cut the scorzonera into 5cm/2 inch pieces. Cook in salted water For 15-20 minutes until just soft. Drain, reserving the stock and set aside.

5. Prick the pastry base with a fork and cover with grease-proof paper. Fill the tin with dried beans and place in the centre of the oven. After 10 minutes, reduce the heat to 190°C/375°F/Gas Mark 5. After a further 5 minutes, remove the beans and the baking paper and put the tin back into the oven.
6. Roll out a lid from the remaining pastry (5mm/ ¼ inch larger than the tin). Decorate with left-over pastry and brush with egg yolk. Slide the lid over the tin, in the oven, and bake until it changes colour. The pastry should not darken.
7. Boil the broccoli florets in a little salted water for a few minutes. Remove from the water and cool in ice-cold water, so that they retain their colour.
8. For the sauce, reduce 500ml/16 fl oz of the scorzonera stock by half. Blend in a liquidiser with the wine and a few pieces of scorzonera. Heat in a saucepan with the crème fraîche, but do not boil. Season with salt and pepper.
9. Add the well-drained scorzonera and broccoli florets, together with the ham, to the sauce. Reheat and pour into the rough puff pastry casing. Cover with the lid and serve immediately.

Recommended drink:
Johannisberg Riesling or a medium dry Müller-Thurgau.

Butter and flour a springform cake tin.

Roll out the puff pastry and use it to line the cake tin.

Cover the pastry case with a layer of greaseproof paper, then fill the tin with dried beans.

Roll out a lid from the remaining pastry and decorate with pastry leftovers.

SCORZONERA FRITTERS

SERVES 6 ■ ■ ■

*Preparation and cooking
time: 1 hour 10 minutes
Kcal per portion: 330
P = 9g, F = 19g, C = 25g*

1kg/2¼lbs scorzonera
salt and pepper
1 tbsp lemon juice
oil for deep frying
lemon wedges to garnish
FOR THE BATTER:
150g/5½oz wholemeal flour
200ml/6 fl oz dry cider
2 egg whites
FOR THE SAUCE:
2 egg yolks
2 tbsps lemon juice
½ tsp Dijon mustard
1 tbsp oil
4 tbsps chopped herbs
100g/4oz quark or curd
  cheese
Worcestershire sauce

1. First make the batter. Sift the flour, mix with the cider until smooth and leave to stand for 1 hour.
2. Wash and peel the scorzonera. Cut into 5cm/2 inch pieces and boil in salted water with 1 tbsp of lemon juice for 15 minutes, until soft. Cool in the liquid.
3. Make the sauce. Mix the egg yolks with the lemon juice and mustard, preferably in a liquidiser. Gradually add the oil. Add the herbs and quark or curd cheese. Season.
4. Whisk the egg whites with a pinch of salt until stiff, then fold into the batter.
5. Heat the oil in a deep-fat fryer or large saucepan to 180°C/350°F.
6. Drain the scorzonera. Dip into the batter and deep-fry in the oil until golden brown. Drain on absorbent paper.
7. Arrange the fritters on a serving platter, garnish with lemon wedges and serve with the sauce.

Recommended drink:
Pinot Noir.

KOHLRABI WITH CHANTERELLES AND MASCARPONE

SERVES 4
Preparation and cooking time: 1 hour
Kcal per portion: 315
P = 10g, F = 24g, C = 14g

750g/1½lbs young kohlrabi
salt and white pepper
300ml/12 fl oz milk
2 shallots
15g/½oz butter
200g/7oz chanterelle
  mushrooms
1 tsp chopped marjoram
150ml/5½ fl oz single cream
2 egg yolks
1 tsp cornflour
75g/3oz mascarpone cheese
pinch of nutmeg

1. Peel the kohlrabi and cut into slices about 5mm/¼ inch thick. Lightly salt the milk, bring to the boil and add the kohlrabi. Boil over a low heat for 10 minutes until half cooked.
2. Heat the butter in a small pan. Chop the shallots and sweat until transparent.
3. Clean and trim the chanterelles; if large, halve lengthways. Add to the kohlrabi and cook gently for 10 minutes.
4. Butter a gratin dish. Drain the kohlrabi and chanterelles; arrange in the dish in layers, finishing with kohlrabi.
5. Heat the oven to 190°C/375°F/Gas Mark 5.
6. Mix together the marjoram, cream, egg yolks, shallots, cornflour and mascarpone; season with salt, pepper and nutmeg. Spread the mixture over the kohlrabi and bake for 30 minutes.
Accompaniment:
fresh crusty bread.
Recommended drink:
Valpolicella.

KOHLRABI STUFFED WITH SAUSAGE

SERVES 4
Preparation and cooking time: 1 hour
Kcal per portion: 300
P = 11g, F = 27g, C = 4g

4 young kohlrabi
200g/7oz pork sausagemeat
2 tbsps finely chopped
  parsley
salt and pepper
butter for the dish
250ml/8 fl oz stock
2 tbsps finely grated Cheddar
  cheese
30g/1oz butter

1. Heat the oven to 180°C/350°F/Gas Mark 4.
2. Peel and carefully hollow out the kohlrabi. Finely chop the flesh and mix with the sausagemeat and half the parsley. Season with salt and pepper.
3. Stuff the kohlrabi with this mixture. Butter a gratin dish generously. Put in the kohlrabi, pour over the stock and cover with a lid or aluminium foil.
4. Bake the kohlrabi for about 35 minutes. At the end of the cooking time remove the lid from the dish, sprinkle the kohlrabi with the cheese and dot with the butter. Return briefly to the oven, then brown under the grill until golden.
Just before serving, sprinkle with the remaining parsley.
Accompaniment:
fresh wholemeal bread.
Recommended drink:
Burgundy or good vin de pays.

CREAMED CARROTS

SERVES 4
Preparation and cooking time: 35-45 minutes
Kcal per portion: 220
P = 3g, F = 18g, C = 13g

1kg/2¼lbs carrots
1 tsp sugar
75g/3oz butter
500ml/16 fl oz stock
2-4 tbsps single cream
salt and pepper
pinch of thyme
2 tbsps finely chopped parsley

1. Scrub young carrots; peel older ones with a swivel peeler. Slice thinly.
2. Melt the sugar and one-third of the butter in a large saucepan. Add the carrots,

> **TIP**
>
> *The purée can be seasoned with chopped chervil. If you are using winter carrots, add a pinch of sugar.*

turn in the butter and cook gently for 3 minutes. Pour in the stock and cook for 20 minutes or until very tender.
3. Drain the carrots. (Reserve the stock, which can be used to make soup.) Purée the carrots in a liquidiser, food processor or vegetable mill.
4. Put the carrot purée in a saucepan, add the cream and season with salt, pepper and thyme.
5. Dice the remaining butter and stir into the hot creamed carrot. Serve sprinkled with the parsley, as a side dish with roasts or grilled meat.

CARROTS IN VERMOUTH SAUCE

SERVES 4
Preparation and cooking time: 30-40 minutes
Kcal per portion: 240
P = 3g, F = 19g, C = 14g

1kg/2¼lbs carrots
45g/1½oz butter
1 tsp sugar
500ml/16 fl oz stock
2 tbsps dry vermouth
125ml/5 fl oz single cream
salt and pepper
pinch of nutmeg

1. Scrub or peel the carrots and slice thinly. Heat the butter in a large saucepan, add the carrots and cook gently for a few minutes, stirring frequently. Pour in the stock, cover and cook slowly for about 15 minutes until slightly soft.
2. Uncover the pan and cook until all the liquid has evaporated.
3. Add the vermouth and the cream. Season with salt and

> **TIP**
>
> *Vermouth gives the sauce a distinctive touch. Serve the carrots sprinkled with chopped parsley, chives or chervil.*

pepper and heat gently until the sauce is creamy.
Serve as a side dish with roast meat or as part of a mixed vegetable dish.

VEGETABLE FLAN

SERVES 6 ■■

*Preparation and cooking
time: 1 hour 5 minutes
Kcal per portion: 360
P = 8g, F = 27g, C = 22g*

300g/10oz carrots
1 head calabrese
2-3 large mushrooms
1 small red pepper
3 small courgettes
salt and pepper
1 tbsp lemon juice
300g/10oz frozen puff pastry,
    thawed
butter for the tin
2 eggs
200ml/7 fl oz single cream
freshly grated nutmeg

1. Scrub or peel the carrots; slice thinly. Divide the calabrese into florets and wipe

TIP

*Hard vegetables
should always be
pre-cooked so
that they take the
same time to
cook as other,
softer vegetables.*

the mushrooms. Wash and quarter the pepper; remove the core and seeds. Slice the flesh into strips. Thinly slice the courgettes.
2. Blanch the vegetables, excluding the mushrooms, in salted water for 3-4 minutes. They should still be firm.
3. Put the lemon juice in a saucepan with a little salted water and blanch the mushrooms briefly. Drain and slice thinly.
4. Butter a springform tin or quiche dish about 30cm/12 inches in diameter. Roll out the pastry and use it to line the tin. Prick all over with a fork.
5. For the glaze, beat the eggs, cream, salt, pepper and nutmeg.

*Finely slice the individual
vegetables, preferably in a food
processor.*

*Arrange the finely sliced
vegetables in concentric rings on
the puff pastry.*

6. Heat the oven to 200°C/400°F/Gas Mark 6.
7. Arrange the carrot slices, overlapping, around the edge of the pastry case. Arrange the courgettes in the same way inside the ring of carrots. Then arrange the remaining vegetables (calabrese florets, strips of pepper and, in the centre, the mushrooms) similarly on the pastry.
8. Bake for 10 minutes. Then pour half the glaze over the flan, bake for 15 minutes, then add the rest. After another 15 minutes remove the flan from the oven. Slide onto a round plate and serve immediately as a hot starter.
Recommended drink:
Beaujolais, mature Burgundy.

STUFFED AUBERGINES AU GRATIN

(see photo on page 31)

SERVES 4 ■■

*Preparation and cooking
time: 20 minutes
Kcal per portion: 260
P = 11g, F = 17g, C = 15g*

4 medium aubergines
salt and pepper
2-3 tbsps oil
150g/5½oz Cheddar cheese
2 large tomatoes
16 basil leaves
8 slices Parma ham

1. Halve the aubergines lengthways. Sprinkle the cut surfaces with a little salt to draw out any bitterness. Leave for about 15 minutes.
2. Meanwhile cut the cheese into 3mm/⅛ inch thick slices. Blanch the tomatoes in boiling water, then peel and slice. Chop eight of the basil leaves into strips.
3. Heat the oven to 220°C/425°F/Gas Mark 7.
4. Line a large baking sheet with aluminium foil and brush with a little oil.
5. Pat the aubergines dry thoroughly with absorbent paper and place, cut sides down, on the sheet. Bake for 20 minutes.
6. Turn the aubergines over and brush the flesh with oil. Cover each half with a slice of ham and 2 slices of tomato. Sprinkle with the basil strips and a little salt. Cover with the cheese slices and return to the oven until the cheese has melted. It should not change colour.

*Halve the aubergines lengthways
and sprinkle with salt.*

*After 15 minutes, pat the cut
surfaces dry with absorbent
paper.*

*Place the aubergines on a baking
sheet, cut surfaces downwards.*

7. Arrange the aubergines on warmed plates. Garnish each half with a basil leaf, sprinkle generously with pepper and serve as a starter.
Recommended drink:
red Côtes de Provence or Côtes-du-Rhône.

RED CABBAGE WITH RED WINE

SERVES 6-8 ■

Preparation and cooking time: 2¼ hours
Kcal per portion (8 portions): 150
P = 3g, F = 10g, C = 7g

1 red cabbage (about 1kg/2¼lbs)
1 large onion
50g/2oz lean rindless bacon
5 tbsps olive oil
200ml/6 fl oz red wine
250ml/8 fl oz stock
1 cooking apple
1 small potato
1 tsp caraway or dill seeds
pinch of sugar
salt and pepper
2 tbsps wine vinegar

1. Finely chop the red cabbage, removing the stalk. Finely dice the onion and bacon.
2. Heat the oil in a large flameproof casserole. Add the onion and bacon and sweat until the onion is transparent. Gradually add the cabbage, stirring frequently. Cook for about 15 minutes, until it collapses.
3. Pour in the red wine. Then add just enough stock to cover the cabbage.
4. Coarsely grate the apple and potato into the cabbage. (The apple can also be cooked whole and added to the finished dish by pressing through a sieve.) Add the caraway or dill seeds, sugar, vinegar, salt and pepper. Cover tightly and simmer gently for about 1½ hours. At the end of the cooking time the liquid should have reduced considerably.
4. Ten minutes before serving, add the vinegar.
5. Serve as an accompaniment to chestnuts, game, poultry or pork.

SAUERKRAUT WITH SPARKLING WINE

(see photo on page 54)

SERVES 4-6 ■

Preparation and cooking time: 1 hour 20 minutes
Kcal per portion (6 portions): 315
P = 5g, F = 27g, C = 6g

1 onion
30g/1oz butter
500g/1lb 2oz bottled sauerkraut
200ml/6 fl oz stock
1 apple
200g/7oz rindless smoked bacon
10 juniper berries
½ tbsp brandy (optional)
250ml/8 fl oz dry sparkling white wine

1. Finely chop the onion. Heat the butter in a large saucepan and sweat the onion until transparent. Add the sauerkraut, fry briefly and pour in the stock.
2. Peel and slice the apple. Chop the bacon and crush the juniper berries lightly.

> **TIP**
>
> *Leftover sauerkraut can be layered with minced roast chicken and cheese sauce and baked.*

Add all to the sauerkraut, cover and cook for at least 1 hour.
3. Thirty minutes before serving turn the sauerkraut mixture into a sieve and drain. Return to the pan with the brandy and sparkling wine; cook until ready.
4. Serve as an accompaniment to roast game.

CHINESE-STYLE CABBAGE

SERVES 4 ■ ■

Preparation and cooking time: 30 minutes
Kcal per portion: 615
P = 30g, F = 47g, C = 14g

500g/1lb2oz pork
2 tbsps peanut oil
½ tsp ground ginger
salt
100ml/3 fl oz strong chicken stock
2 tbsps sake or dry sherry
2 leeks
750g/1½lbs Chinese leaves
1 tsp sugar
3 tbsps soy sauce
1 garlic clove
pinch of cayenne

1. Slice the meat into thin strips. Heat 1 tablespoon of oil in a wok or deep frying-pan and stir-fry the meat briefly over a high heat. Season with ginger and salt. Add 2 tablespoons of chicken stock and the sake or sherry. Reduce the heat and stir-fry for a further 15 minutes.
2. Meanwhile trim and wash the leeks; slice into rings.
3. Heat 1 tablespoon of oil in another frying-pan and sweat the leeks for a few minutes.
4. Wash and drain the Chinese leaves. Cut into 2cm/¾ inch strips and add to the leeks. Stir-fry until tender-crisp and remove from the pan.
5. Add the sugar, soy sauce, crushed garlic and remaining chicken stock to the frying-pan and quickly bring to the boil.
6. Add the vegetables and sauce to the meat and season with cayenne.

Accompaniment:
rice.
Recommended drink:
rosé wine.

PEAS WITH HAM AND PEPPER

SERVES 4 ■

Preparation and cooking time: 30 minutes
Kcal per portion: 175
P = 12g, F = 8g, C = 15g

100g/4oz cooked ham
1 small onion
1 green pepper
1 tbsp olive oil
400g/14oz frozen peas, thawed
4 canned tomatoes
1 garlic clove
salt and pepper

1. Dice the ham and finely chop the onion. Halve, core and de-seed the pepper; cut into small squares.
2. Heat the olive oil in a frying-pan and gently cook the ham, onion, pepper and peas for 10 minutes.

> **TIP**
>
> *These vegetables can be transformed into an excellent pasta dish when mixed with 125ml/5 fl oz single cream and 2 tbsps grated Parmesan. Bring to the boil and serve mixed with freshly cooked ribbon pasta.*

3. Chop the tomatoes. Add to the braised vegetables, together with the crushed garlic, and cook for 5 minutes.
4. Season with salt and pepper and serve immediately as a side dish.

Wholefood Recipes

*W*holefood cuisine revels in making the most of each season's vegetables, using the right herbs and spices with each dish so that delicious aromas issue from every pot and pan. Fresh, crisp vegetables are essential, perfectly prepared so that every dish brings out each unmistakable flavour.
Why not try for yourself the Celeriac Pancakes with Tomatoes, Chard Strudel Stuffed with Vegetables and Cracked Wheat, or Mushroom Patties with Chervil Sauce. You will soon realise why wholefood cooking is becoming so popular.

Courgette and Mushroom Terrine (see recipe on page 75)

SPANISH ONIONS WITH ASIAN STUFFING

SERVES 4 ■■
Preparation and cooking time: 1½ hours
Kcal per portion: 300
P = 5g, F = 14g, C = 34g

4 Spanish onions
1 medium carrot
100g/4oz celery
45g/1½oz butter
salt and pepper
150g/5½oz shiitake
    mushrooms
250ml/8 fl oz strong beef
    stock
1 tbsp chopped fresh ginger
3 tbsps sake
2 tsps soy sauce
1½ tbsps sherry vinegar
100g/4oz boiled basmati rice

1. Peel the onions and cut a lid from the top. Make incisions across the inside of the onion with a knife, taking

The best way to hollow out the onions is to use a small scoop; failing that use a teaspoon.

Peel or scrub the carrot and dice it very finely.

TIP

Basmati rice comes from India and has a particularly delicate flavour. It takes about 20 minutes to boil. Ordinary long-grain rice can be used instead.

care not to pierce the outer two layers of the onion. Hollow out the insides using a teaspoon and chop finely.
2. Peel or scrub the carrot. Trim, wash and finely dice the celery stalks.
3. Heat half the butter in a casserole and lightly brown the onion, carrot and celery. Season with salt and pepper.
4. Finely chop the mushrooms. Heat the remaining butter in a small pan add the mushrooms and brown them lightly. Season with salt and pepper.

5. Bring the stock to the boil with the ginger, sake, soy sauce and sherry vinegar.
6. Heat the oven to 200°C/400°F/Gas Mark 6.
7. Thoroughly mix the rice, vegetable mixture, mushrooms and sauce. Season again with salt and pepper.
8. Butter a baking dish. Put the hollowed-out onions in the dish and stuff with the rice mixture. Cover with aluminium foil and bake for 45 minutes. After 30 minutes, uncover and continue cooking until the onions are tender.

CHEESE-TOPPED SPINACH DUMPLINGS

SERVES 4 ■■
Preparation and cooking time: 45 minutes
Kcal per portion: 415
P = 29g, F = 29g, C = 9g

750g/1½lbs spinach
salt and pepper
250g/8oz quark or curd
    cheese
3 egg yolks
2-3 tbsps wholemeal flour
freshly grated nutmeg
200g/7oz Cheddar cheese,
    grated
butter for the dish

1. Carefully sort the spinach and wash thoroughly. Bring a saucepan of well-salted water to the boil. Blanch the spinach for 1 minute, then drain in a colander. Squeeze out well and chop finely.
2. Put the quark or curd cheese into a bowl and mix thoroughly with the spinach, egg yolks and enough flour to make a firm dough. Season well with salt, pepper and nutmeg.
3. Bring a large saucepan of well-salted water to the boil and heat the grill to high. Butter a large heatproof dish.
4. Using a spoon, make dumplings from the spinach mixture and cook for 2-3 minutes in the gently boiling salted water. Remove using a slotted spoon. Drain and place side by side in the dish. Sprinkle with cheese and brown quickly under the grill.
Serve as an accompaniment to fish dishes or as a hot snack served with a cheese sauce.

AUBERGINES AU GRATIN

SERVES 4 ■
Preparation and cooking time: 45 minutes
Kcal per portion: 485
P = 22g, F = 38g, C = 11g

2 medium aubergines (about
    750g/1½lbs)
salt and white pepper
6 tbsps olive oil
4 large beefsteak tomatoes
2 tbsps chopped basil leaves
1 tsp oregano
400g/14oz Mozzarella cheese

1. Wash the aubergines and remove the stalk ends. Cut lengthways into slices about 1cm/½ inch thick. Sprinkle with salt and leave to stand for 15 minutes.
2. Blanch the tomatoes. Peel and cut into thick slices.
3. Heat the oven to 200°C/400°F/Gas Mark 6.
4. Squeeze out the aubergine slices thoroughly and dry on absorbent paper. Heat 4 tablespoons of oil in a non-stick frying-pan. Quickly brown the aubergine slices on both sides. Place side by side on a baking sheet.
5. Cover the aubergine slices with the tomato slices. Sprinkle with salt, pepper, basil and oregano. Thinly slice the Mozzarella and lay on top. Drizzle over the remaining olive oil and bake in the centre of the oven for 15 minutes. Switch on the grill and quickly brown the aubergines.
An accompaniment to fish dishes or a hot starter.
Recommended drink:
light, aromatic red wine, e.g. Chianti Classico or Dolcetto.

RED LENTILS IN RICE PAPER

SERVES 4 ■■
*Preparation and cooking
time: 1 hour
Soaking time: a few hours
Kcal per portion: 360
P = 15g, F = 19g, C = 29g*

*200g/7oz split red lentils
1 tsp turmeric
4 sheets rice paper
1 red onion, finely diced
2 garlic cloves
50g/2oz fresh ginger root
1 green chilli
2 tbsps oil
250ml/8 fl oz stock (beef,
    chicken or vegetable)
2 tbsps dry sherry
2 tbsps sherry vinegar
2 tbsps soy sauce
salt and pepper
cumin
100g/4oz yoghurt
oil for the dish
1 egg yolk*

*Soak the sheets of rice paper in
cold water until they turn milky
white.*

*Before baking, brush the parcels
with beaten egg yolk.*

1. Cook the lentils with the
turmeric in a generous
amount of water until tender. Drain thoroughly in a
sieve.
2. Soak the sheets of rice
paper in cold water until
they turn milky white.
Remove carefully and
spread them out next to one
another on a tea towel.
3. Peel the garlic and ginger.
Core and de-seed the chilli.
Dice all three finely.
4. Heat the oil in a flameproof casserole and lightly
brown the garlic, ginger and
chilli. Add the lentils and
pour in the stock, sherry,
vinegar and soy sauce.
5. Season with salt, pepper
and a pinch of cumin. Cook
over a medium heat until
almost all the liquid has
evaporated, then remove
from the heat and stir in the
yoghurt.
6. Heat the oven to
200°C/400°F/Gas Mark 6.
7. Spread the lentil mixture
over the rice paper. Fold the
side edges over the filling,
then fold lengthways. Butter
a baking sheet and put the
parcels on it. Brush with
beaten egg yolk and bake in
the centre of the oven for 10
minutes or until golden.
Serve as a starter.
Recommended drink:
Prosecco di Valdobbiadene
or a spicy aperitif wine such
as Traminer or Moscato; fruit
juice.

CHEESE-TOPPED LENTIL PATTIES

SERVES 4 ■
*Preparation and cooking
time: 30 minutes
Kcal per portion: 715
P = 30g, F = 55g, C = 24g*

*1 small leek
2 medium carrots (about
    200g/7oz)
5-6 tbsps oil
150g/5½oz cooked lentils
50g/2oz chopped walnuts
100g/4oz crème fraîche
2 eggs
salt and pepper
200g/7oz Cheddar cheese,
    grated*

1. Cut the roots and dark
green parts from the leek.
Halve the leek lengthways
and wash thoroughly in running water. Peel or scrub the
carrots. Finely dice both
vegetables.
2. Heat 2 tablespoons of the
oil in a flameproof casserole.
Gently fry the vegetables,
then stir in the lentils.
Remove from the heat and
cool the mixture.
3. When cool, stir in the walnuts, crème fraîche and
eggs. Season with salt and
pepper and shape into small
patties.
4. Heat the grill to high.
5. Heat the remaining oil in a
non-stick frying-pan. Fry the
patties for about 2 minutes
on each side over a medium
heat.
6. Drain the patties on
absorbent paper. Put them
on a heatproof plate.
Sprinkle with grated cheese
and brown under the grill.
Accompaniment:
mixed salad and herby
cheese sauce.
Recommended drink:
Müller-Thurgau or another
aromatic white wine.

CELERIAC PAN-CAKES WITH TOMATOES

SERVES 4 ■
*Preparation and cooking
time: 30 minutes
Kcal per portion: 460
P = 21g, F = 36g, C = 12g*

*400g/14oz celeriac
2 tbsps milk
3 eggs
45g/1½oz wholemeal flour
50g/2oz chopped hazelnuts
salt and pepper
freshly grated nutmeg
4-6 tbsps oil
4 small firm tomatoes
125g/5oz grated Parmesan
    cheese*

1. Peel the celeriac and grate
coarsely. Add the milk and
eggs, then stir in the flour
and nuts. Mix well and season with salt, pepper and
nutmeg.
2. Line a baking sheet with
greaseproof paper.
3. Heat a little oil in a non-
stick frying-pan. Using a
ladle, pour in a little of the
celeriac mixture. Swirl evenly over the base of the pan
and fry on both sides until
brown. Make the remaining
mixture into pancakes in the
same way. Place the cooked
pancakes on a baking sheet
lined with greaseproof
paper.
4. Heat the grill to high.
5. Slice the tomatoes.
Arrange on top of the pancakes and sprinkle with
cheese. Quickly brown
under the grill,
The pancakes are also excellent made with courgettes or
cauliflower.
An accompaniment to meat
dishes.

CRACKED WHEAT AND COURGETTE RISSOLES

SERVES 4 ■■

*Preparation and cooking
time: 50 minutes
Kcal per portion: 580
P = 19g, F = 22g, C = 77g*

600g/1¼lbs small courgettes
salt and pepper
200g/7oz cracked wheat
4 slices wholemeal bread
bunch of spring onions
2 garlic cloves
½ tsp rosemary
1 tsp thyme
2 eggs
breadcrumbs
4-5 tbsps oil

*The best way to grate courgettes
is in a food processor.*

1. Cut the ends off the courgettes, wash and coarsely
grate. Sprinkle with salt and
leave to stand for 30 minutes.
2. Cook the cracked wheat
in the pressure-cooker, covered in water, for 15 minutes.
Soak the slices of bread in
lukewarm water.

*Finely slice the spring onions,
including some of the green
parts.*

TIP

*If you do not
have a pressure-
cooker, it is better
to soak the
cracked wheat in
cold water for a
few hours, then
boil them in a
saucepan for 25-
30 minutes until
tender but still
firm.*

3. Trim and wash the spring
onions. Slice finely, including
some of the green parts.
Finely chop the garlic.
4. Squeeze out the courgettes and slices of bread
thoroughly. Put into a bowl.
Thoroughly drain the
cracked wheat in a sieve.
Add to the courgettes and

*Fry the rissoles in oil on both
sides for 3-4 minutes.*

bread, together with the
spring onion, garlic and
herbs. Gradually add the
eggs. Season with salt and
pepper and work into a soft
dough. If it is too wet, bind
with breadcrumbs.
5. Heat the oil in a non-stick
frying-pan. Fry the rissoles
over a medium heat for 3-4
minutes on each side.
Accompaniment:
cheese sauce.

SPANISH ONIONS WITH SOUFFLE STUFFING

SERVES 2 ■■

*Preparation and cooking
time: 1½ hours
Kcal per portion: 730
P = 47g, F = 48g, C = 28g*

4 Spanish onions
butter for the dish

FOR THE STUFFING:
125ml/5 fl oz single cream
200g/7oz curd cheese
100g/4oz grated Parmesan
    cheese
3 eggs, separated
salt and white pepper
freshly grated nutmeg

1. Heat the oven to
200°C/400°F/Gas Mark 6.
Bake the onions, un-peeled,
for 1 hour.
2. Cool and peel the onions.
Cut a lid from the top and
hollow out the centre, leaving three layers of onion
intact. Butter an ovenproof
dish and put the onions in it.
3. For the stuffing, finely
blend the onion flesh and
the cream in a liquidiser.
Press through a sieve and
mix with the curd cheese,
Parmesan and egg yolks.
Season with salt and pepper.
Whisk the egg whites stiffly
and fold into the mixture.
Stuff the onions and bake in
the centre of the oven for 15
minutes.
An accompaniment to any
meat dish. Also makes a
good starter.

COURGETTE AND MUSHROOM TERRINE

(see photo on page 68)

SERVES 4 ■■

*Preparation and cooking
time: 1 hour 20 minutes
Kcal per portion: 460
P = 14g, F = 40g, C = 13g*

500g/1lb2oz small courgettes
200g/7oz mushrooms
2 small shallots
45g/1½oz butter
250ml/8 fl oz single cream
250ml/8 fl oz milk
4 eggs
bunch of parsley
salt and white pepper
freshly grated nutmeg

1. Wash the courgettes, trim
and slice thinly. Wipe the
mushrooms and slice thinly.
Finely dice the shallots.
2. Heat the butter in a
flameproof casserole and
lightly brown the vegetables.
3. Heat the oven to
200°C/400°F/Gas Mark 6.
4. Thoroughly whisk together the cream, milk and eggs.
Finely chop the parsley, add
to the mixture and season
with salt, pepper and nutmeg. Add the vegetables.
Butter a 1.5-litre/2½-pint terrine (or line with greaseproof
paper) and fill with the mixture. Bake in the centre of
the oven for about 45 minutes.
The terrine looks very attractive if it is made in a round,
dome-shaped dish and cov-
ered with slices of lightly
cooked courgette after turning out.
Excellent hot or cold.
Recommended drink:
strong, full-bodied white
wine, e.g. Pinot Bianco from
Friuli.

CHARD STRUDEL STUFFED WITH VEGETABLES AND CRACKED WHEAT

SERVES 4 ■ ■
Preparation and cooking time: 1 hour 10 minutes
Kcal per portion: 420
P = 21g, F = 20g, C = 39g

200g/7oz cracked wheat
400g/14oz mixed vegetables
   (leeks, carrots, courgettes,
   kohlrabi)
10 large chard leaves
salt and white pepper
2 shallots
30g/1oz butter
freshly grated nutmeg
200g/7oz quark or curd
   cheese
4 eggs

1. Cook the cracked wheat, covered in water, in a pressure-cooker for 15 minutes. Discard the water and drain.
2. Trim and wash the vegetables and cut into fine strips. Separate the chard stalks from the leaves. Finely slice the stalks and add to the other vegetables.
3. Bring a generous amount of salted water to the boil. First blanch the mixed vegetables for 2 minutes, then the chard leaves for 30 seconds. Drain the leaves. Spread them out next to each other, slightly overlapping, on a large piece of greased aluminium foil.
4. Dice the shallots finely. Heat the butter in a large frying-pan, add the onion and sweat until transparent. Add the drained vegetables. Cook for a few minutes, then season with salt, pepper and nutmeg.
5. In a bowl, mix the quark or curd cheese with the eggs. Add the cracked wheat and the vegetables. Mix well and season generously.
6. Spread the mixture over the chard leaves and roll the

Spread the chard out on a large piece of aluminium foil, with the leaves just overlapping.

Spread the quark mixture evenly over the chard leaves.

Wrap the chard leaf strudel tightly in aluminium foil.

leaves up into a strudel. Wrap tightly in the aluminium foil and cook in lightly simmering salted water for 15 minutes. Serve hot cut into thick slices.
Accompaniment: sherry or port sauce.

BRUSSELS SPROUT LEAVES IN CREAMY SAUCE

SERVES 4 ■
Preparation and cooking time: 30 minutes
Kcal per portion: 340
P = 6g, F = 31g, C = 8g

500g/1lb2oz Brussels sprouts
salt and white pepper
250ml/8 fl oz single cream
3 tbsps white port
50g/2oz butter
freshly grated nutmeg

1. Trim and wash the Brussels sprouts. Separate the individual leaves. Bring a large amount of salted water to the boil and blanch the leaves for about 1 minute. Drain in a sieve.
2. Bring the cream, port and butter to the boil in a high-sided frying-pan or shallow flameproof casserole. Season with salt, pepper and nutmeg and cook until reduced a little.
3. Put the Brussels sprout leaves into the cream sauce and toss gently. Serve immediately.
An accompaniment to white meat, rabbit and poultry, as well as game dishes in a white sauce.

> **TIP**
>
> *Use fairly large sprouts for this dish. The firmer and more tightly closed the sprouts, the better they are.*

CHARD TOPPED WITH PARMESAN

SERVES 4 ■
Preparation and cooking time: 30 minutes
Kcal per portion: 310
P = 14g, F = 27g, C = 3g

12 large chard leaves
125ml/4 fl oz beef stock
200ml/7 fl oz single cream
salt and pepper
freshly grated nutmeg
125g/5oz grated Parmesan
   cheese
2 egg yolks

1. Wash the chard leaves. Cut out the stalks and slice both the stalks and the leaves into thin strips, keeping them separate.
2. Bring the stock to the boil in a flameproof casserole and briefly poach the chard stalks. Pour in just under half

> **TIP**
>
> *Chard stalks and leaves take widely varying times to cook, so always cook the stalks first, then just heat the leaves.*

the cream and simmer until reduced by a third. Add the leaf strips and cook for about 1 minute. Season with salt, pepper and nutmeg.
3. Heat the grill to high.
4. Put the chard mixture into an ovenproof dish and sprinkle over a thick layer of Parmesan. Whisk the egg yolks with the remaining cream and pour evenly over the cheese. Brown quickly under the grill.
An accompaniment to poultry and game.

MUSHROOM PATTIES WITH CHERVIL SAUCE

SERVES 4 ■■
Preparation and cooking time: 45 minutes
Kcal per portion: 640
P = 13g, F = 56g, C = 21g

FOR THE PATTIES:
1 Spanish onion
300g/10oz mushrooms
oil for frying
100g/4oz cooked whole oats
2 tbsps chopped flat-leaved parsley
3 eggs
salt and white pepper
wholemeal flour if needed

FOR THE SAUCE:
250ml/8 fl oz stock (vegetable, beef or chicken)
125ml/5 fl oz single cream
50g/2oz butter
salt and white pepper
2 tbsps whipped cream
50g/2oz fresh chervil

1. Finely dice the onion. Wipe or peel the mushrooms and finely dice.
2. Heat 2 tablespoons of oil in a frying-pan. Gently sweat the onion without allowing it to change colour.
3. Combine the onions, mushrooms, oats and parsley in a bowl. Gradually add the eggs. Season with salt and pepper and work into a soft dough If it is too soft add a little flour.
4. For the sauce, heat the stock, cream and butter in a saucepan. Season with salt and pepper and cook until reduced by a third.
5. Make small patties from the mushroom mixture. Heat 4-6 tablespoons oil in a non-stick frying-pan. Fry the patties for 3-4 minutes on each side.
6. Meanwhile finely chop the chervil, reserving a few springs to garnish. Beat the reduced sauce with a hand-held mixer, adding the whipped cream and

If liked, peel the mushrooms with a pointed knife.

Just before serving, mix the whipped cream and chervil into the sauce.

chopped chervil. Pour the sauce over the patties and garnish with chervil.
Accompaniment:
glazed carrots or broccoli florets.

ASPARAGUS AND WHOLE-WHEAT GRAINS TOPPED WITH PARMESAN

SERVES 4 ■■
Preparation and cooking time: 45 minutes
Kcal per portion: 455
P = 23g, F = 28g, C = 36g

2kg/4½lbs asparagus
salt and white pepper
1 tsp sugar
30g/1oz butter
1 tbsp chopped shallot
125g/5oz cooked wholewheat grains
100g/4oz grated Parmesan cheese
125ml/5 fl oz single cream
2 egg yolks

1. Scrape the asparagus stalks and cut off the lower ends if necessary. Bring a generous amount of salted, sugared water to the boil. Boil the spears for 5-10 minutes, depending on thickness, until still firm. Drain well.
2. Heat the butter in a frying-pan. Gently fry the shallot and wholewheat grains. Season with salt and pepper.
3. Heat the grill to high.
4. Transfer the asparagus spears into an ovenproof dish. Sprinkle first with wholewheat grains, then with Parmesan.
5. Beat the cream with the egg yolks and pour over the cheese. Quickly brown the asparagus under the grill.
Recommended drink:
dry Grey Burgundy from Franconia or Baden.

LEEKS TOPPED WITH GORGONZOLA

SERVES 4 ■■
Preparation and cooking time: 45 minutes
Kcal per portion: 375
P = 15g, F = 31g, C = 10g

4 young leeks
salt and white pepper
1 medium carrot
30g/1oz butter
100ml/4 fl oz single cream
freshly grated nutmeg
150g/5½oz Gorgonzola cheese
2 egg yolks
butter for the dish

1. Trim off the roots, remove and reserve the green parts from the leeks. Cut in half, wash thoroughly and blanch in boiling salted water for about 3 minutes. Remove and drain well.
2. Trim, wash and finely dice the carrot, together with the green parts of the leeks. Heat the butter in a flame-proof casserole and sweat the diced vegetables. Season with salt and pepper.
3. Heat the oven to 200°C/400°F/Gas Mark 6.
4. Bring the cream, salt, pepper and nutmeg to the boil in a saucepan. Press the Gorgonzola through a sieve into the cream. Bring back to the boil, then remove from the heat and beat in the egg yolks.
5. Butter an ovenproof dish and put in the leeks. Cover with the diced vegetables. Pour over the cream. and bake in the centre of the oven for about 15 minutes or until cooked.
An accompaniment to roast beef or veal.

QUARK AND VEGETABLE STRUDEL

SERVES 4 ■ ■ ■

Preparation and cooking time: 50 minutes
Relaxing time: 2 hours
Kcal per portion: 1085
$P = 41g, F = 77g, C = 56g$

FOR THE PASTRY:
300g/10oz wholemeal flour
pinch of salt
1 egg
1 egg yolk
125g/5oz crème fraîche
75g/3oz butter
1 egg yolk
4 tbsps single cream

FOR THE FILLING:
100g/4oz kohlrabi
100g/4oz carrots
100g/4oz courgettes
500g/1lb2oz quark or curd cheese
4 eggs
2 tbsps chopped kohlrabi leaves
2 tbsps chopped carrot leaves
100g/4oz roast pistachio nuts
white pepper
freshly grated nutmeg

1. For the pastry, sift the flour and salt on to the work top. Make a hollow in the centre. Place the egg, egg yolk and cream in the hollow. Dot the butter, in small knobs, around the edge. Using a round-bladed knife, first cut the fat into the flour. Quickly knead to a smooth dough, working from the outside inwards. Wrap in foil and chill for 2 hours.
2. For the filling, peel the kohlrabi and carrot. Cut the ends from the courgettes. Chop everything into thin sticks. Blanch in plenty of boiling salted water and drain thoroughly in a sieve.
3. Put the quark or curd cheese into a bowl. Stir until smooth and gradually add the eggs, chopped kohlrabi and carrot leaves, pistachio nuts and drained vegetables.

Season with salt, pepper and nutmeg.
4. Heat the oven to 200°C/400°F/Gas Mark 6.
5. Roll out the dough on a floured board into as thin a square as possible. Cover with the quark and vegetable mixture and roll up.

> **TIP**
>
> *The strudel can be served either as a side dish or as a main course, possibly with a herb sauce. Toasted sunflower seeds can be added to the quark mixture instead of roasted pistachio nuts.*

6. Butter a baking sheet and put the strudel on it with the join underneath. Heat together the egg yolks and cream. Brush the strudel with the mixture. Bake in the centre of the oven for 15-20 minutes until golden.
Recommended drink:
dry Sylvaner.

Put the quark, eggs, pistachio nuts and chopped leaves into a bowl and stir.

Stir the vegetables into the quark mixture.

Spread the quark and vegetable mixture over the rolled-out pastry.

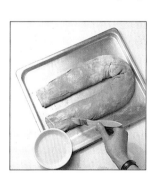

Before baking, brush the strudel with a mixture of egg yolk and cream.

BAKED POTATOES WITH MUSHROOM FILLING

SERVES 4 ■

Preparation and cooking time: 1 hour 10 minutes
Kcal per portion: 345
$P = 7g, f = 24g, C = 25g$

4 large floury potatoes
200g/7oz mushrooms
1 shallot
45g/1½oz butter
150g/5½oz crème fraîche
salt and white pepper
150g/5½oz fresh bean sprouts

1. Heat the oven to 200°C/400°F/Gas Mark 6. Thoroughly wash the potatoes and wrap, unpeeled, in aluminium foil. Bake for about 1 hour, until cooked.
2. Meanwhile wipe and finely chop the mushrooms;

> **TIP**
>
> *The potatoes look attractive served in the open aluminium foil. In summer, the potato parcels can also be barbecued.*

finely dice the shallot. Heat the butter in a frying-pan, add the mushrooms and shallot and brown lightly over a medium heat. Stir in the crème fraîche. Season with salt and pepper and bring to the boil. Add the bean sprouts and heat quickly in the mushroom sauce.
3. Take the potatoes out of the oven. Unwrap and cut off a lid. Hollow out the potatoes a little and fill with the mushroom mixture.

Quick-and-easy Recipes

*T*he quick recipes in this chapter are proof that there's no magic about fast food. Barely half an hour is all that's needed to produce an attractively served vegetable side-dish or main course. Aubergines with Garlic, Curried Chinese Leaves with Almonds, Cheese-topped Fennel with a nut crust: all can become complete meals for those who are happy not to eat meat, particularly when complemented by a bowl of salad or a nourishing dessert. If time is short frozen vegetables can be used instead of fresh ones, making the preparation and cooking times even quicker.

Aubergines with Garlic
(see recipe on page 84)

AUBERGINES WITH GARLIC

(see photo on page 83)

SERVES 4 ■
*Preparation and cooking
time: 30 minutes
Kcal per portion: 225
P = 3g, f = 19g, C = 10g*

*600g/1¼lbs aubergines
5 tbsps olive oil
4 garlic cloves
500g/1lb2oz canned chopped
    tomato
salt and pepper
2 tsps thyme, fresh or dried*

1. Wash the aubergines and remove the stalk ends. First quarter lengthways, then cut into slices about 1cm/½ inch thick. Heat the olive oil in a large frying-pan. and fry until golden. Remove from the pan.
2. Crush the garlic and stir into the oil remaining in the pan. Sweat until golden.

> ### TIP
> *This vegetable dish also tastes delicious cold. It could then be seasoned with a little red wine vinegar or lemon juice.*

3. Add the tomatoes and cook over a high heat until reduced by a third.
4. Return the aubergines to the frying-pan. Season with salt, pepper and thyme and cook for a further 10 minutes.
For a complete meal add 500g/1lb2oz minced steak and serve with potatoes.
An accompaniment to leg of lamb or chicken.

CAULIFLOWER WITH HAZELNUT BUTTER

SERVES 4 ■
*Preparation and cooking
time: 30 minutes
Kcal per portion: 385
P = 6g, F = 38g, C = 6g*

*1 medium cauliflower (about
    750g/1½lbs)
salt and pepper
juice of ½ lemon
125g/5oz butter
5 tbsps ground hazelnuts
freshly grated nutmeg*

1. Remove any leaves from the cauliflower, divide it into the smallest possible florets and wash.
2. Bring a generous amount of water, seasoned with salt and lemon juice, to the boil. Add the cauliflower florets, bring to the boil, then simmer for 8 minutes, until still firm.
3. Melt the butter in a flameproof casserole. Sprinkle in the ground hazelnuts and cook until the butter foams. Season with salt, pepper and nutmeg.
4. Using a slotted spoon, remove the cauliflower from the cooking liquid and drain thoroughly. Arrange on a plate and pour over the hot hazelnut butter. Serve immediately.
Almonds, walnuts or pistachio nuts can be used instead of hazelnuts.
Gorgonzola cream sauce also goes very well with cauliflower, instead of the nut butter, with scrambled eggs and ham as an accompaniment.
Serve with game.

CURRIED CHINESE LEAVES WITH ALMONDS

SERVES 4 ■
*Preparation and cooking
time: 25 minutes
Kcal per portion: 195
P = 6g, F = 14g, C = 11g*

*1 large onion
2 tbsps oil
1 head Chinese leaves (about
    1kg/2¼lbs)
3 garlic cloves
salt and pepper
2 tbsps curry powder
750g/1½lb can tomatoes
2 tbsps flaked almonds
15g/½oz butter
1 bunch coriander or flat-
    leaved parsley*

1. Chop the onion. Heat the oil in a large frying-pan and sweat the onion until transparent.
2. Meanwhile quarter the Chinese leaves lengthways, remove the stalk and slice across into 5mm/¼ inch strips. Wash and drain well.
3. Crush the garlic, add to the chopped onion and sweat briefly. Add the Chinese leaves. Cook, covered, for 3 minutes.
4. Season the vegetables with salt and pepper. Sprinkle with the curry powder. Add the tomatoes, together with the juice. Cover and cook for 10 minutes over a low heat.
5. Meanwhile heat the butter in a non-stick frying-pan and stir-fry the almonds until golden.
6. Rinse the coriander or parsley, pull off the leaves, pat dry, and just before serving, sprinkle over the curried Chinese leaves together with the almonds.
Accompaniment:
rice, preferably a mixture of long-grain and wild rice.
Recommended drink:
buttermilk.

BROCCOLI WITH SMOKED PORK

SERVES 4 ■
*Preparation and cooking
time: 25 minutes
Kcal per portion: 175
P = 14g, F = 12g, C = 2g*

*600g/1¼lbs broccoli, fresh or
    frozen
salt and pepper
1 tbsp oil
1 medium onion
200g/7oz thickly sliced
    smoked pork
freshly grated nutmeg*

1. Trim fresh broccoli, divide into florets and wash. Slice the stalks. Thaw frozen broccoli and cut into small florets.
2. Bring a large saucepan of salted water to the boil and cook the broccoli for 7 minutes so that it is still firm.

> ### TIP
> *Without the pork the broccoli also makes a good side dish with fish and poultry. The pork can be replaced by prawns and the vegetables served with fish dishes.*

Cool in ice-cold water and drain well.
3. Meanwhile heat the oil in a large high-sided frying-pan. Chop the onion and sweat until transparent.
4. Finely dice the pork. Add to the frying-pan with the broccoli. Season with salt, pepper and nutmeg. Cover and cook for a further 7 minutes.
An accompaniment to meat balls or potato pancakes.

CHARD WITH BALSAMIC VINEGAR

SERVES 4 ■
Preparation and cooking time: 25 minutes
Kcal per portion: 155
P = 4g, F = 13g, C = 6g

750g/1½lbs chard
30g/1oz butter
3 garlic cloves
salt and pepper
generous pinch of cayenne
4 tbsps crème fraîche
2 tbsps balsamic vinegar or
   1 tbsp red wine vinegar

1. Wash the chard and cut off the end of the stalks. Cut or pull the leaves from the stalks. Slice the stalks into 1cm/½ inch strips.

TIP

Chard makes a good starter, either hot or cold.

2. Heat the butter in a large frying-pan. Add the stalk strips and sweat, covered, over a low heat for 8 minutes.
3. Crush the garlic, and add to the stalks. Stir in the chard leaves. Season with salt, pepper and cayenne.
4. Add the crème fraîche and vinegar. Stir and bring to the boil.
The vegetables can be sprinkled with toasted pine nuts or grated Parmesan.
Accompaniment:
to poached eggs served with mashed potato and lots of chives. Also tasty with Parma ham or cold roast beef.

Cut off the end of the chard stalks.

Cut out the hard leaf end.

Slice the chard stalks into 1cm/½ inch strips.

First sweat the tender stalk strips in butter over a low heat. Then stir in the green leaves.

CREAMY LEEKS TOPPED WITH CHEESE

SERVES 4 ■
Preparation and cooking time: 30 minutes
Kcal per portion: 460
P = 19g, f = 39g, C = 9g

750g/1½lbs leeks
salt and white pepper
butter for the dish
freshly grated nutmeg
250g/8oz quark or curd
   cheese
200ml/7 fl oz single cream
6 tbsps grated Gouda cheese
3 tbsps sunflower seeds

1. Trim the leeks and cut off the ends. Slit lengthways and rinse well under cold running water.
2. Heat the oven to 240°C/475°F/Gas Mark 9.
3. Cut the leeks diagonally into 1cm/½ inch pieces. Blanch for 3 minutes in boiling salted water. Cool in ice-cold water and drain well in a sieve.
4. Butter a large shallow baking dish and arrange the leeks in it. Season with salt, pepper and nutmeg.
5. In a bowl, mix together the quark or curd cheese, cream, grated cheese and sunflower seeds. Season with salt, pepper and nutmeg; spread over the leeks. Bake in the centre of the oven for 15 minutes until golden.
Accompaniment:
mashed potato with lots of chives. Serves 8 as a starter, browned in individual dishes.
Recommended drink:
white wine spritzer.

CHEESE-TOPPED FENNEL WITH A NUT CRUST

SERVES 2 ■
Preparation and cooking time: 30 minutes
Kcal per portion: 1145
P = 37g, F = 98g, C = 29g

750g/1½lbs fennel bulbs
salt and pepper
butter for the dish
200g/7oz crème fraîche
150g/5½oz grated Gouda
   cheese
100g/4oz ground hazelnuts
freshly ground black pepper

1. Wash the fennel bulbs. Cut off and reserve any leaves. Cut the bulbs lengthways into slices about 1cm/½ inch thick.
2. Cook the fennel in boiling salted water for 3 minutes. Remove using a slotted spoon and drain well.
3. Heat the oven to 220°C/425°F/Gas Mark 7.
4. Butter a large ovenproof dish and arrange the fennel slices so that they overlap.
5. Put the crème fraîche into a bowl. Add the cheese and hazelnuts and mix together. Season well with salt and pepper. Spread evenly over the fennel.
6. Bake in the centre of the oven for 15 minutes, until golden. Sprinkle with reserved fennel leaves.
This dish can be made more substantial by sandwiching well-mashed canned tuna between the fennel slices. Pistachio nuts can be used instead of hazelnuts.
Accompaniment:
French bread or mashed potato.
Recommended drink:
light white wine from Friuli or Verdicchio.

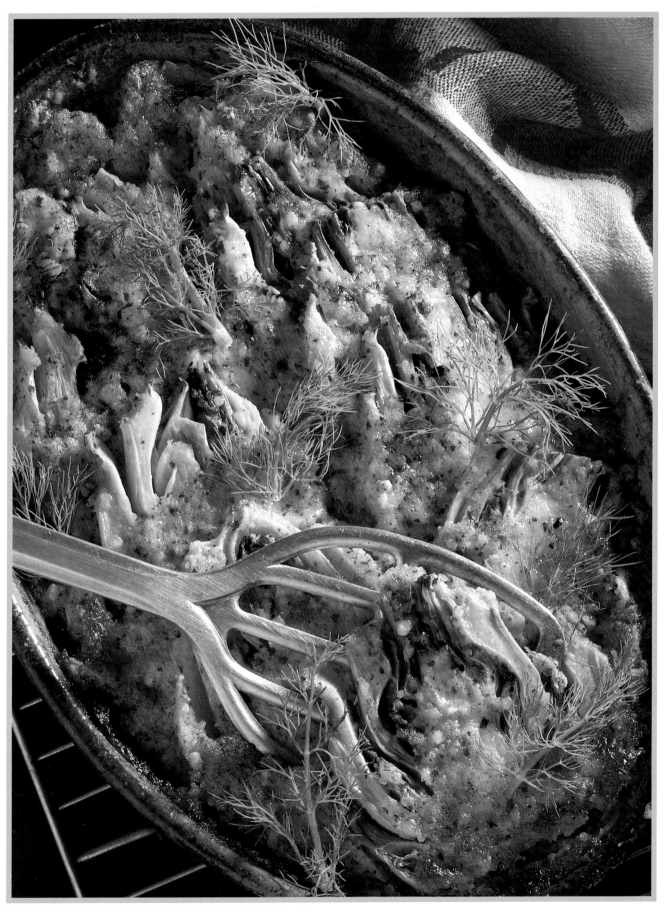

BRAISED ASPARAGUS IN CHERVIL SAUCE

SERVES 2 ▪
Preparation and cooking time: 30 minutes
Kcal per portion: 380
P = 15g, F = 30g, C = 18g

1kg/2¼lbs asparagus
45g/1½oz butter
salt and white pepper
juice of 1 lemon
2 tbsps maple syrup
100g/4oz chervil
2 egg yolks
300g/10oz yoghurt

1. Scrape the lower part of the asparagus stalks and cut off the ends. Cut the stalks diagonally into pieces about 4cm/1½ inches long. Set the tips to one side.
2. Heat the butter in a large frying-pan. Sweat the asparagus, covered, without the tips, for 15 minutes over a medium heat. After 5 minutes, add salt and pepper. Drizzle with lemon juice and maple syrup.
3. Meanwhile rinse the chervil, pat dry and snip off the stalks. Reserve a few sprigs for garnishing. Blend the remaining chervil in a liquidiser with the egg yolks and yoghurt, to make a smooth sauce. Season with salt and pepper.
4. About 5 minutes before the end of the cooking time, add the asparagus tips to the frying-pan.
5. Arrange the asparagus on four warmed plates, with a dollop of sauce in the centre. Garnish with chervil leaves.
Accompaniment: new potatoes. This quantity serves four as a side dish and is tasty with poached salmon.
Recommended drink: claret.

STIR-FRIED ASPARAGUS

SERVES 4 ▪
Preparation and cooking time: 30 minutes
Kcal per portion: 315
P = 7g, f = 28g, C = 8g

500g/1lb2oz asparagus
250g/8oz mange-tout
salt
3 tbsps oil
3 tbsps sesame seeds
3 tbsps soy sauce
1 tbsp very dry sherry
1 punnet mustard and cress

1. Peel only the lower third of the asparagus and cut off the ends of the stalks. Wash briefly and chop into 3cm/1½ inch pieces. Wash the mange-tout and snip off the ends.
2. Blanch the asparagus in boiling salted water for 3 minutes. Cool in ice-cold water and drain. Do the same with the mange-tout, but blanch for only 1 minute.
3. Heat the oil in a wok or large frying-pan. Fry the sesame seeds until golden, stirring constantly.
4. Add the asparagus and the mange-tout peas. Cook for 5 minutes over a low heat, stirring constantly. Drizzle with the soy sauce and sherry.
5. Rinse the mustard and cress under running water. Using kitchen scissors, snip the leaves over the vegetables and stir in.
An accompaniment to fillet of veal or grilled salmon. Can also be served as a vegetarian main course for two, with brown rice or new potatoes.

KOHLRABI IN GORGONZOLA SAUCE

SERVES 4 ▪
Preparation and cooking time: 25 minutes
Kcal per portion: 520
P = 23g, F = 44g, C = 8g

6 kohlrabi (about 750g/1½lbs)
salt and pepper
butter for the dish
250ml/8 fl oz single cream
300g/10oz Gorgonzola cheese
freshly grated nutmeg
lemon juice
1 bunch chervil

1. Peel the kohlrabi and halve it. Slice it thinly, preferably in a food processor or using a mandolin. Put the slices in a saucepan with boiling salted water and cook for 3 minutes. Remove with a slotted spoon and drain well.
2. Heat the oven to 220°C/425°F/Gas Mark 7.
3. Butter a large ovenproof dish and arrange the kohlrabi slices so that they overlap.
4. Bring the cream to the boil in a small saucepan. Add the Gorgonzola and melt, stirring constantly. Season with salt, pepper, nutmeg and lemon juice.
5. Rinse the chervil and pat dry. Pull the leaves from the stalks and sprinkle most of them over the kohlrabi slices. Pour over the sauce and brown in the centre of the oven for 10 minutes.
6. Before serving sprinkle with the reserved chervil leaves.
An accompaniment to medallions of veal or poached egg. Can also be served as a vegetarian main course for two with potatoes or sesame rice.

SWEET AND SOUR CARROTS

SERVES 4 ▪
Preparation and cooking time: 30 minutes
Kcal per portion: 150
P = 2g, F = 10g, C = 14g

750g/1½lbs carrots
salt and pepper
45g/1½oz butter
3 tbsps maple syrup
juice of 1 lemon
pinch of cumin
1 carton mustard and cress

1. Peel the carrots and cut diagonally into 1cm/½ inch thick slices. Put into a saucepan, just cover with

> **TIP**
>
> *Half of the carrots can be replaced by courgettes. Use fresh mint instead of mustard and cress for an unusual flavour.*

water, add salt and bring to the boil. Cook for 8 minutes over a low heat.
2. Tip the carrots into a sieve and drain well.
3. Heat the butter in a large frying-pan. Add the maple syrup and bring to the boil. Add the carrots and sweat for 5 minutes. Sprinkle with the lemon juice. Season with salt, pepper and cumin.
4. Rinse the mustard and cress under running water. Snip the leaves directly into the frying-pan.
An accompaniment to cold roast beef or roast chicken. Can also be served as a starter on a bed of fresh spinach, sprinkled with toasted sesame seeds.

MIXED PEPPERS WITH SAUSAGE

SERVES 4 ■
Preparation and cooking time: 25 minutes
Kcal per portion: 805
P = 32g, F = 55g, C = 44g

1 large onion
2 tbsps olive oil
750g/1½lbs mixed red, green
   and yellow peppers
125ml/4 fl oz tomato juice
salt and pepper
1 tsp paprika
generous pinch of cayenne
250g/8oz kabanos or
   peperone sausage
l bunch flat-leaved parsley

1. Slice the onion into thin rings. Heat the olive oil in a large frying-pan and sweat the onion rings until transparent.
2. Halve, core, de-seed and wash the peppers. Slice across into narrow strips and add to the frying-pan. Pour in the tomato juice. Season with salt, pepper, paprika and cayenne. Cook gently for 15 minutes.
3. Skin the sausage and slice, not too thickly. Combine with the vegetables and cook for 5 minutes.
4. Rinse, pat dry and roughly chop the parsley. Just before serving, mix with the other ingredients.
Instead of spicy sausage, you could use cooked ham, sliced into strips.
Accompaniment: mashed potato.
Recommended drink: light red wine, e.g. Chianti or Beaujolais-Villages.

Halve the peppers lengthways. Remove the core and seeds, then wash.

Thinly slice the pepper halves.

Pour the tomato juice over the strips of pepper, season and cook for 15 minutes.

Peel and slice the sausage. Add to the vegetables and heat for a further 5 minutes.

COURGETTES WITH TURKEY STRIPS

SERVES 2 ■
Preparation and cooking time: 30 minutes
Kcal per portion: 420
P = 55g, F = 18g, C = 9g

400g/14oz turkey fillet
30g/1oz butter
salt and white pepper
freshly grated nutmeg
450g/1lb courgettes
3 garlic cloves
250ml/8 fl oz vegetable stock
1 bunch flat-leaved parsley

1. Slice the turkey into thin strips.
2. Heat the butter in a large frying-pan. Fry the turkey strips over a high heat until golden brown. Season with salt and pepper, sprinkle with nutmeg and set aside.
3. Cut the stalk ends from the courgettes. Wash and slice directly into the butter remaining in the pan. Cook gently until golden.
4. Crush the garlic and add to the courgette slices.
5. Pour in the stock and bring to the boil. Add salt and pepper. Cover and cook gently for 5 minutes.
6. Meanwhile rinse, pat dry and roughly chop the parsley. Add the turkey strips to the courgette slices, with their meat juices and reheat briefly.
7. Just before serving stir in the parsley.
Chicken or pork can be used instead of the turkey fillets.
Accompaniment: mashed potato.
Recommended drink: dry cider.

MUSHROOM FRITTATA

SERVES 4 ■ ■
Preparation and cooking time: 30 minutes
Kcal per portion: 250
P = 13g, F = 20g, C = 4g

1 medium onion
3 tbsps olive oil
750g/1½lbs oyster or button
   mushrooms
2 garlic cloves
salt and pepper
1 bunch chives
5 eggs

1. Heat the oil in a medium-sized high-sided frying-pan. Finely dice the onion and sweat over a low heat until transparent.
2. Meanwhile, wipe the mushrooms and slice finely. Add to the frying-pan and sweat for 10 minutes over a medium heat. Crush the garlic and add to the pan; season with salt and pepper.
3. Finely chop the chives. Beat the eggs and stir in the chives. Pour over the mushrooms. Allow to set over a low heat, shaking the pan from time to time so that the mixture does not stick.
4. After about 7 minutes, slide the frittata on to a lid or plate. Turn and slide back into the frying-pan and fry for a further 10 minutes, until cooked.
The frittata looks attractive cut into portions like a cake. It can also be served cold as a starter.
Accompaniment: tomato salad with spring onions.

SAVOY CABBAGE WITH SESAME SEEDS AND BEAN SPROUTS

(see photo on page 21)

SERVES 4 ■
Preparation and cooking time: 30 minutes
Kcal per portion: 180
P = 6g, F = 16g, C = 4g

300g/10oz Savoy cabbage
250g/8oz mushrooms
3 tbsps soya oil
2 garlic cloves
2 tbsps sesame seeds
150g/5½oz fresh bean sprouts
salt and pepper
generous pinch of cayenne
3 tbsps dry sherry
3 tbsps soy sauce

1. Remove the thick outer leaves from the cabbage. Quarter the cabbage and cut out the thick central stalk. Cut the quarters crossways into 5mm/¼ inch strips. Wash and drain.
2. Wipe and trim the mushrooms. Using an egg slicer, slice finely.
3. Heat the soya oil in a wok or large high-sided frying-pan. Fry the mushrooms briefly. Crush the garlic and add to the pan. Add the strips of cabbage and sprinkle with the sesame seeds.
4. Briefly rinse the bean sprouts and add to the cabbage.
5. Season the vegetables with salt, pepper and cayenne. Pour in the sherry and soy sauce. Cover and cook for 10 minutes over a medium heat.
This dish can be enhanced by browning some minced meat with the mushrooms – about 100g/4oz per person.
Accompaniment: rice.
Recommended drink: dry sherry.

SPINACH WITH FETA AND PINE NUTS

SERVES 4 ■
Preparation and cooking time: 30 minutes
Kcal per portion: 445
P = 14g, F = 41g, C = 6g

600g/1¼lbs spinach, fresh or frozen
1 small onion
2 tbsps olive oil
3 garlic cloves
4 tbsps pine nuts
salt and pepper
1 tsp oregano
300g/10oz Feta cheese

1. Wash fresh spinach and snip off the stalks. Remove frozen spinach from its packaging.
2. Chop the onion finely. Heat the oil in a large saucepan, add the onion and sweat until transparent.
3. Crush the garlic cloves and add to the onion. Add the spinach and sweat for 10 minutes.
4. Sprinkle with the pine nuts. Season with salt, pepper and oregano.
5. Finely dice the Feta or crumble it between your fingers. Sprinkle over the spinach and cook for 5 minutes over a very low heat.
Instead of pine nuts, flaked almonds can be used.
An accompaniment to grilled lamb chops.

MANGE-TOUT WITH LEMON SAUCE

SERVES 4 ■
Preparation and cooking time: 20 minutes
Kcal per portion: 325
P = 9g, F = 24g, C = 17g

600g/1¼lbs mange-tout
salt and white pepper
1 small onion
15g/½oz butter
1 tbsp very dry sherry
200g/7oz crème fraîche
juice of ½ lemon
2 spring onions (optional)

1. Wash the mange-tout and snip off the ends. Blanch in boiling salted water for 1 minute. Cool in ice-cold water and drain well.
2. Finely chop the onion. Heat the butter in a large saucepan and sweat the

> ### TIP
> *If serving this dish as a starter the mange-tout can be combined with 200g/7oz prawns. Then it makes enough to serve 8.*

onion until transparent. Pour in the sherry and heat until reduced almost completely.
3. Add the crème fraîche and lemon juice. Cook gently for 3 minutes, then season with salt and pepper.
4. Add the mange-tout to the sauce and heat for 5 minutes.
5. Optional: chop two spring onions into rings and stir into the dish.
Accompaniment: buttered rice.
Recommended drink: Schillerwein from Baden-Württemberg or rosé.

SPRING CABBAGE IN SHERRY CREAM SAUCE

SERVES 4 ■
Preparation and cooking time: 25 minutes
Kcal per portion: 410
P = 5g, F = 35g, C = 8g

1 small spring cabbage (450g/1lb)
4 spring onions
30g/1oz butter
5 tbsps very dry sherry
250ml/8 fl oz double cream
1 tbsp Worcestershire sauce
salt and white pepper
2 tbsps sunflower seeds

1. Trim and quarter the cabbage, removing the thick central stalk. Cut the quarters crossways into very fine strips. Wash and drain thoroughly.
2. Trim and wash the spring onions. Chop into fine rings.
3. Heat the butter in a large saucepan and sweat the onions. Add the spring cabbage and fry, stirring, for 5 minutes.
4. Pour in the sherry, then stir in the cream. Season with Worcestershire sauce, salt and pepper. Cover and simmer over a medium heat for 10 minutes.
5. Meanwhile dry-fry the sunflower seeds in a non-stick frying-pan until golden. Taste the vegetables and season again if necessary. Sprinkle over the sunflower seeds.
The sherry can be replaced by white wine or sparkling wine. Pumpkin seeds can be used instead of sunflower seeds.
An accompaniment to fillet of veal or steamed shellfish, such as scampi.

Microwave Recipes

*Q*uick preparation and short but gentle cooking – that's the beauty of a microwave oven, whether you are cooking Celery in White Wine, Asparagus with Mange-tout or hearty Hungarian Potato Goulash. There is simply no better way of cooking tender vegetables. The delicious flavours of the dishes contained in this chapter are an integral part of the microwave cooking programme. For best results remember that vegetable dishes prepared in the microwave oven have to be stirred once during cooking, that it is better to use several small containers than one large one and that round rather than rectangular cooking dishes are best.

Okra with Tomatoes
(see recipe on page 100)

MULTI-COLOURED VEGETABLE STEW

SERVES 4 ■■
Microwave alone
Preparation and cooking time: 1 hour
Kcal per portion: 425
P = 5g, F = 32g, C = 23g

1 small aubergine
salt and pepper
2 small courgettes
1 red pepper
1 yellow pepper
400g/14oz floury potatoes
2 onions
2 garlic cloves
375g/12oz canned tomatoes
1 sprig thyme
1 sprig rosemary
125ml/4 fl oz olive oil
125ml/4 fl oz dry red wine

Sprinkle the aubergine slices with salt and leave for 30 minutes.

1. Remove the stalk end from the aubergine. Wash and chop the aubergine into 5mm/¼ inch slices. Sprinkle with salt and leave for about 30 minutes.
2. Meanwhile wash the courgettes and peppers. Remove the stalk ends from the cour-

Slice the courgettes and chop the peppers into strips.

TIP

This dish can be made with different combinations of vegetables, depending on the time of year.

Season the mixed vegetables. Place in a microwave dish and pour over the oil and wine.

gettes. Peel and wash the potatoes. Slice both vegetables. Halve, core and deseed the peppers; slice into fine strips. Finely chop the onions and garlic.
3. Squeeze out the aubergine slices. Arrange in alternating layers with the other vegetables in a large microwave dish. Chop the tomatoes and pour over the other vegetables with the juice. Add the herbs, salt and

pepper. Pour over the oil and wine. Cover and cook for 26-30 minutes at 600 watts. Uncover for the last 10 minutes.
4. Leave the vegetables to stand for a short time. Mix carefully and remove the herb sprigs.
Serve with grilled meat or fish.

ORIENTAL-STYLE STUFFED PEPPERS

SERVES 4 ■■
Microwave alone
Preparation and cooking time: 1 hour
Kcal per portion: 680
P = 7g, F = 47g, C = 46g

8 yellow peppers
2 onions
8 tbsps olive oil
150g/5½oz uncooked long-grain rice
salt and pepper
50g/2oz currants
8-10 fresh mint leaves
½ bunch parsley
50g/2oz toasted pine nuts
1 tsp ground cinnamon
generous pinch ground cloves
grated zest of ½ lemon
570ml/1 pint passata (sieved tomato)
2 tbsps dry white wine

1. Wash the peppers. Cut a lid from the stalk ends and carefully remove the seeds and cores. Brush a microwave baking dish with 1 tbsp oil. Place the peppers in the dish.
2. Dice the onions and put with 3 tablespoons of oil in a microwave dish. Fry for 3-4 minutes at 600 watts. Then stir in the rice, add salt and brown for 2 minutes at 600 watts.
3. Put the currants in the microwave, covered, with 4 tbsps water for 2 minutes at 600 watts. Leave to stand for a few minutes longer.
4. Finely chop the mint and parsley. Add to the rice, together with the pine nuts and drained currants. Season with the cinnamon and cloves.
5. Stuff the peppers with the rice mixture. Do not fill more than two-thirds full as the rice will swell. Replace the lids cut from the peppers. Mix the passata with 5 tbsps oil and the wine. Pour into the dish.

Mix the pine nuts, currants, herbs and spices with the lightly cooked rice.

Only stuff the peppers two-thirds full with the rice mixture as the rice will swell.

6. Cover and cook for 10 minutes at 600 watts and for 20 minutes at 180 watts. During this time, turn the dish once through 180 degrees.
In Turkey, stuffed peppers are also served cold as a meze (starter).
Cooking in the microwave does not really save time in this recipe, but it helps preserve the strong individual flavours.
Recommended drink:
light, dry white wine, e.g. Verdicchio Classico.

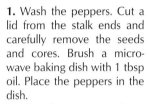

HUNGARIAN POTATO GOULASH

SERVES 4 ■
Microwave alone
Preparation and cooking
time: 40 minutes
Kcal per portion: 295
P = 5g, F = 20g, C = 23g

600g/1¼lbs waxy potatoes
2 red peppers
2 large onions
50g/2oz rindless smoked
   streaky bacon
2 tbsps oil
salt and pepper
1 tbsps paprika
1 tsp caraway seeds
2 sprigs marjoram
250ml/8 fl oz strong beef
   stock
3 tbsps soured cream
½ bunch parsley

1. Peel, wash and finely dice the potatoes. Wash and halve the peppers; remove cores and seeds. Dice into 1cm/½ inch squares. Finely chop the onions.
2. Finely dice the bacon. Place in a microwave dish with the oil. Brown for 3-4 minutes at 600 watts.
3. Add the diced vegetables. Season with salt, pepper, paprika, caraway and the marjoram leaves. Pour in the stock. Cover and cook for 17-20 minutes at 600 watts, stirring from time to time.
4. Stir the cream into the vegetables and cook, uncovered, for 4-5 minutes at 600 watts, until thickened.
5. Chop the parsley and sprinkle over the dish. Leave to stand for a few minutes before serving. For a spicier flavour, add finely chopped chillies.
An accompaniment to sausages or fried chops.

CREAMY POTATOES

SERVES 4 ■
Microwave alone
Preparation and cooking
time: 30 minutes
Kcal per portion: 485
P = 6g, F= 38g, C = 29g

750g/1½lbs floury potatoes
1 onion
1 garlic clove
30g/1oz butter
salt and white pepper
freshly grated nutmeg
400ml/14 fl oz single cream
a few chervil leaves

1. Peel and wash the potatoes. Chop into 1cm/½ inch cubes. Finely dice the garlic. Put both into a microwave dish with the butter. Fry for 2-3 minutes at 600 watts, until transparent.
2. Add the diced potato and season with salt, pepper and

> ### TIP
> *The potato pieces should be about the same size so that they cook evenly. Do not forget to reset the microwave after stirring.*

nutmeg. Pour in the cream. Cover and cook for 15-18 minutes at 600 watts. After 5 minutes, uncover, stir once and finish cooking uncovered.
3. Sprinkle the chervil leaves over the dish. Leave to stand for a few minutes longer.
Serve with rissoles or sausages.

BAVARIAN CABBAGE

SERVES 4 ■
Microwave alone
Preparation and cooking
time: 40 minutes
Kcal per portion: 180
P = 3g, F = 16g, C = 6g

½ head white cabbage
   (400g/14oz trimmed)
50g/2oz rindless smoked
   streaky bacon
2 tbsps oil
1 tsp sugar
1 tsp caraway seeds
250ml/8 fl oz ham stock
1 tbsp white wine vinegar
salt and pepper

1. Cut the stalk from the white cabbage. Remove limp outer leaves. Wash the cabbage and slice into thin strips.
2. Finely dice the bacon. Put in a large microwave dish with oil and sugar. Glaze for 4-5 minutes at 600 watts, stirring once.
3. Add the white cabbage, stir well and sprinkle with caraway seeds. The cabbage should not be piled too high. Pour in the stock and vinegar. Cover and cook for 15-18 minutes at 600 watts. Uncover, stir and finish cooking uncovered. Leave to stand for a few more minutes before serving. Season with salt and pepper if needed. After about 10 minutes of the cooking time, thicken, if desired, with a little flour and water.
Serve with grilled sausages or roast pheasant.

KOHLRABI WITH GARDEN PEAS

SERVES 4 ■
Microwave alone
Preparation and cooking
time: 30 minutes
Kcal per portion: 140
P = 4g, F = 9g, C = 8g

3 young kohlrabi with leaves
1 small onion
45g/1½oz butter
5 tbsps dry white wine
salt and white pepper
150g/5½oz fresh shelled peas
1 tbsp chopped parsley

1. Remove the leaves from the kohlrabi. Reserve the tender inner leaves. Peel the bulbs, cut into thin slices and then into strips.
2. Chop the onion and put into a microwave dish with 20g/¾oz butter. Fry,

> ### TIP
> *Frozen peas can be used instead of fresh ones, and crème fraîche in place of butter.*

uncovered, for 2 minutes at 600 watts. Add the strips of kohlrabi and pour in the wine. Season with salt and pepper. Cover and cook for 6-8 minutes at 600 watts, stirring once.
3. Add the peas, cover, and cook for a further 3-4 minutes at 600 watts.
4. Carefully cut the kohlrabi leaves into thin strips. Stir into the vegetables with the remaining butter and the parsley.
An accompaniment to roast veal.

EXOTIC LENTILS

SERVES 4 ■
*Microwave alone
Preparation and cooking
time: 30 minutes
Soaking time: a few hours
Kcal per portion: 300
P = 8g, F = 19g, C = 20g*

*125g/5oz green lentils
1 large carrot
2 celery stalks
1 onion
1-2 garlic cloves
4 tbsps oil
125ml/4 fl oz dry white wine
salt and pepper
2 sprigs thyme
1 bay leaf
2 tbsps crème fraîche
1 tbsp chopped parsley*

*Place the finely chopped
vegetables and the oil in a
microwave dish.*

*Mix the soaked, drained lentils
with the browned vegetables and
pour in the white wine.*

*After half of the cooking time, stir
in the crème fraîche.*

1. Cover the lentils with plenty of cold water and soak for 4 hours.
2. Trim and wash the carrot and celery; dice very finely. Chop the onion and the garlic finely. Put them all into a large microwave dish with the oil. Brown for 5 minutes at 600 watts, stirring once.
3. Drain the lentils and add to the dish. Pour in the white wine and season with salt and pepper. Add the thyme and bay leaf. Cover and cook for 6-8 minutes at 600 watts, stirring from time to time.
4. Uncover and stir the crème fraîche into the vegetables. Reduce, uncovered, for a further 4-5 minutes at 600 watts.
5. Remove the herbs and leave the vegetables to stand for a few minutes longer. Serve sprinkled with parsley. To make the dish creamier, blend some of the lentils in a liquidiser.
An accompaniment to pork or Polish sausage.

OKRA WITH TOMATOES

(see photo on page 95)

SERVES 4 ■ ■
*Microwave alone
Preparation and cooking
time: 45 minutes
Kcal per portion: 280
P = 9g, F = 24g, C = 32g*

*400g/14oz okra
2 tbsps white wine vinegar
salt and pepper
1 onion
1 garlic clove
6 tbsps olive oil
500g/1lb2oz beefsteak
    tomatoes
2 sprigs thyme
125ml/4 fl oz white wine
2 tbsps chopped parsley*

*Carefully remove the tops of the
okra with a sharp knife.*

*Put the okra on a shallow dish,
drizzle with vinegar and sprinkle
with salt. Leave to marinate for 30
minutes.*

*Stir the okra into the tomato
sauce.*

1. Wash the okra. Carefully remove the ends, using a sharp knife. Take care not to damage the flesh. Arrange side by side on a rectangular plate. Drizzle with vinegar and sprinkle with salt. Leave for at least 30 minutes.
2. Meanwhile finely chop the onion and garlic. Put them with the oil in a microwave dish. Fry for 2 minutes at 600 watts, until transparent.
3. Wash the tomatoes. Cut a cross in the top and put, dripping wet, in a microwave dish. Put them in the microwave for 2-3 minutes at 600 watts. Rinse in cold water. Then peel, seed, chop and add to the onion. Add the thyme, salt and pepper. Pour in the white wine. Cook gently, uncovered, for 6-8 minutes at 600 watts.
4. Mix the okra with the tomato sauce, cover and cook for 6-8 minutes at 600 watts, stirring once gently. Leave to stand for a few minutes longer. Serve sprinkled with parsley.
An accompaniment to roast chicken or grilled fish.

ONIONS STUFFED WITH VEAL

SERVES 2　■■
*Microwave alone
Preparation and cooking
time: 50 minutes
Kcal per portion: 595
P = 28g, F = 37g, C = 32g*

2 Spanish onions
200g/4oz minced veal
2 tbsps uncooked rice
1 tbsp chopped parsley
2 tbsps tomato purée
salt and pepper
1 tsp paprika
100g/4oz crème fraîche
2 tbsps oil
5 tbsps dry white wine

1. Peel the onions. Place in a microwave dish with 250ml/8 fl oz water. Cover and cook for 4-5 minutes at 600 watts, turning once.
2. Mix together the veal, rice, parsley and 1 tablespoon of tomato purée. Season with salt, pepper and ¼ tsp paprika.
3. Cut a lid from the onions. Hollow out the inner flesh with a teaspoon. Leave at least two layers around the outside. Finely chop the onion flesh and mix half of it with the meat mixture. Stuff the onions with the mixture and put in a microwave dish.
4. Stir together the crème fraîche, oil, wine, remaining tomato purée and paprika. Pour a little of the mixture over each onion. Distribute the rest, with the remaining onion, around the onions.
5. Cover and cook for 20-25 minutes at 600 watts.
Recommended drink: lager.

BEETROOT WITH HORSERADISH

SERVES 4　■
*Microwave alone
Preparation and cooking
time: 35 minutes
Kcal per portion: 130
P = 2g, F = 8g, C = 12g*

500g/1lb2oz raw beetroot
1 onion
45g/1½oz butter
salt and pepper
2 tbsps freshly grated
　horseradish
1 tbsp balsamic vinegar
1 tbsp maple syrup

1. Wash, peel and coarsely grate the beetroot. Dice the onion finely and put with the butter in a microwave dish. Fry, uncovered, for 2 min-

Peel the beetroot and grate coarsely in a food processor.

utes at 600 watts, until transparent.
2. Add the beetroot, salt and pepper. Cover and cook for 8 minutes at 600 watts.
3. Stir the horseradish, vinegar and syrup into the vegetables. Cook, uncovered, for a further 4-6 minutes at 600 watts.
An accompaniment to boiled beef.

LEEK AND BACON

SERVES 4　■
*Microwave alone
Preparation and cooking
time: 25 minutes
Kcal per portion: 275
P = 4g, F = 27g, C = 4g*

2 large leeks (about
　500g/1lb2oz)
75g/3oz rindless smoked
　streaky bacon
1 tbsp oil
salt and white pepper
generous pinch of stock
　granules
freshly grated nutmeg
125ml/5 fl oz single cream
1 tbsp lemon juice

1. Remove the roots from the leeks. Cut off almost all the green parts. Halve the leeks lengthways, wash thoroughly and cut into 5mm/¼ inch slices.
2. Finely dice the bacon. Put the bacon and the oil into a large microwave dish. Fry, uncovered, for 3-4 minutes at 600 watts, until the fat is transparent.
3. Add the leeks. They should not be piled too high. Season with salt, pepper, stock granules and nutmeg; pour in the cream. Cover and cook for 8-10 minutes at 600 watts. After 5 minutes, uncover, stir and continue cooking uncovered. Season with the lemon juice.
An accompaniment to sausages or boiled beef.

MIXED PEPPERS

SERVES 4　■
*Microwave alone
Preparation and cooking
time: 40 minutes
Kcal per portion: 225
P = 3g, F = 19g, C = 10g*

2 small red peppers
2 small yellow peppers
2 small green peppers
1 Spanish onion
1 garlic clove
2 large beefsteak tomatoes
5 tbsps olive oil
2 sprigs thyme
1 bay leaf
salt and pepper
1 tbsp chopped parsley

1. Halve, core and de-seed the peppers. Slice the flesh into thin strips. finely dice the garlic.

TIP

This dish can be enhanced by adding green or black olives.

2. Cut a cross in the top of the tomatoes. Wash and put in a microwave dish dripping wet. Put in the microwave for 3-4 minutes at 600 watts. Cool in cold water, peel and halve. Remove the stalk ends and seeds.
3. Place all the vegetables in a large microwave dish. Do not pile too high. Pour over the oil. Add the herbs and season with salt and pepper. Cover and cook for 18-20 minutes at 600 watts, stirring from time to time.
4. Remove the herbs and sprinkle with parsley.
An accompaniment to boiled beef or steak.

ASPARAGUS WITH MANGE-TOUT

SERVES 4 ■
Microwave alone
Preparation and cooking
time: 40 minutes
Kcal per portion: 95
P = 5g, F = 7g, C = 7g

500g/1lb2oz white asparagus
125ml/4 fl oz water
pinch of sugar
salt
30g/1oz butter
200g/7oz mange-tout
a few sprigs of chervil
a little grated orange zest

1. Peel the asparagus stalks. Cut off the ends and chop into 5cm/2 inch pieces. Reserve the tips. Place the

> **TIP**
>
> *The thickness of the asparagus spears and its quality determine how long it will take to cook.*

rest in a microwave dish. Pour in the water. Add salt, sprinkle with sugar and add 10g/¼oz butter. Cover and cook for 5-6 minutes at 600 watts.
2. Meanwhile, snip the ends off the mange-tout and wash. Mix the mange-tout and asparagus tips with the rest of the asparagus. Cover and cook for a further 4-5 minutes at 600 watts.
3. Pull off the chervil leaves. Mix into the vegetables, together with the orange zest and remaining butter. Leave to stand, covered, for a few minutes longer.
An accompaniment to veal or turkey steak, baked plaice or sole.

Carefully peel the asparagus spears, using an asparagus peeler or swivel vegetable peeler.

Mix the mange-tout with the pre-cooked asparagus.

Before serving, mix orange zest, chervil leaves and butter into the vegetables.

SCORZONERA IN CARAWAY SAUCE

SERVES 2 ■
Microwave alone
Preparation and cooking
time: 1 hour
Kcal per portion: 340
P = 5g, F = 32g, C = 7g

1l/1¾ pints water
2 tbsps vinegar
500g/1lb2oz scorzonera
salt and white pepper
1 tbsp caraway seeds
200ml/7 fl oz single cream
1 tsp balsamic vinegar
juice and zest of ½ lemon
1 tbsp chopped parsley

1. Put the water and vinegar into a large bowl. Wash and peel the scorzonera. Place in the bowl of water and vinegar so that it does not discolour.
2. Chop the scorzonera into even-sized pieces. Place in a microwave dish and pour in 250ml/8 fl oz water. Add salt and half the caraway seeds.
3. Cover and cook for 20-25 minutes at 600 watts. At the end of the cooking time, remove the vegetables from the microwave. Leave to stand, covered, for a few more minutes.
4. During this time put the cream, the remaining caraway seeds, vinegar, lemon juice and zest, salt and pepper in a microwave dish. Reduce by half for 8-10 minutes at 600 watts, until smooth.
5. Drain the scorzonera in a sieve and mix into the cream sauce. Heat, uncovered, for 3-4 minutes. Serve sprinkled with parsley.
An accompaniment to roast beef, steak or escalopes.

CELERY IN WHITE WINE

SERVES 2 ■
Microwave alone
Preparation and cooking
time: 30 minutes
Kcal per portion: 280
P = 3g, F = 21g, C = 8g

1 head celery (about
*   500g/1lb2oz)*
2 shallots
50g/2oz butter
salt and white pepper
125ml/4 fl oz dry white wine
½ tsp flour
1 tbsp chopped herbs (parsley,
*   basil, tarragon, chives)*

1. Trim the celery. Cut off any leaves and reserve. Separate the stalks and wash. Chop into 2cm/¾ inch pieces.
2. Dice the shallots and put in a microwave dish with 20g/¾oz butter. Fry for 2 minutes at 600 watts until transparent. Then add the celery. Season with salt and pepper. Pour in the white wine. Cover and cook for 10 minutes at 600 watts.
3. Knead the remaining butter with the flour. Stir into the vegetables. Reduce, uncovered, for 4-5 minutes at 600 watts.
Serve sprinkled with herbs and finely chopped celery leaves.
An accompaniment to braised dishes or sweetcorn rissoles.

> **TIP**
>
> *In a conventional oven, this would take twice as long to cook.*

GREEK-STYLE MUSHROOMS

SERVES 2 ■
*Microwave alone
Preparation and cooking
time: 25 minutes
Kcal per portion: 305
P = 7g, F = 23g, C = 6g*

*500g/1lb2oz mushrooms
2 small onions
1 bay leaf
1 sprig thyme
generous pinch of coriander
juice of ½ lemon
3 tbsps olive oil
125ml/4 fl oz dry white wine
salt and white pepper
1 tbsp chopped parsley*

1. Wipe the mushrooms and slice. Finely dice the onions. Put both in a microwave dish and add the bay leaf, thyme and coriander. Pour in the lemon juice, oil and wine. Season with salt and pepper.

> ### TIP
> *Mushrooms cooked in this way also taste delicious as a cold starter. Brown mushrooms have a stronger, more aromatic flavour than white ones.*

2. Cover and put into the microwave for 15 minutes at 600 watts, stirring once during this time.
3. Remove the herbs. Stir the parsley into the mushrooms and serve.
An accompaniment to quick-fried meat or grills.

Wipe the mushrooms and cut off the stalk ends.

Place all the ingredients in a microwave dish; they will only need to cook for 15 minutes.

Take care when removing the mushrooms from the oven – the bowl will be very hot.

SWISS-STYLE CARROT PURÉE

SERVES 4 ■
*Microwave alone
Preparation and cooking
time: 35 minutes
Kcal per portion: 225
P = 3g, F = 16g, C = 16g*

*300g/10oz floury potatoes
500g/1lb2oz carrots
125ml/5 fl oz single cream
salt
pinch of sugar
30g/1oz butter
2 tbsps finely chopped chervil*

1. Peel, wash and finely chop the potatoes and carrots. Put in a microwave dish with the cream. Add the salt and sugar. Cover and cook for 15-18 minutes at 600 watts, stirring from time to time.

> ### TIP
> *If you can get young, bunched carrots in the spring, make sure they have fresh, juicy leaves. Remove the leaves immediately since they draw the juice out of the carrots.*

2. Blend the potato and carrot mixture in a liquidiser. Stir in the butter in small knobs. Put the carrot purée into a bowl and sprinkle with chervil.
An accompaniment to braised beef or sausages.

COURGETTES WITH TOMATO

SERVES 2 ■
*Microwave alone
Preparation and cooking
time: 30 minutes
Kcal per portion: 265
P = 6g, F = 23g, C = 8g*

*2 courgettes (about 250g/8oz)
200g/4oz button mushrooms
2 beefsteak tomatoes
2 shallots
1 tbsp oil
20g/¾oz butter
1 sprig thyme
salt and pepper
½ tsp paprika
2 tbsps crème fraîche
2 tbsps chopped parsley*

1. Wash the courgettes and cut off the ends. Wipe the mushrooms. Slice both vegetables finely.
2. Cut a cross in the top of the tomatoes. Place dripping wet in a microwave dish, cover and put in the microwave for 2-3 minutes at 600 watts. Then rinse in cold water, peel and dice finely, without the stalk ends and seeds.
3. Finely chop shallots and put with the oil and butter in a microwave dish. Fry for 2 minutes at 600 watts, until transparent.
4. Add the sliced courgettes and mushrooms. Sprinkle with individual thyme leaves. Season with salt, pepper and paprika. Stir in the crème fraîche, cover and cook for 4 minutes at 600 watts.
5. Add the diced tomato. Stir and cook, uncovered, for a further 4-5 minutes at 600 watts.
6. Sprinkle with parsley and leave to stand for a little while longer before serving. An accompaniment to rissoles or quick-fried meat.

Lean Cuisine

*A*s far as vegetables are concerned lean cuisine has an added advantage. Eating light healthy food does not mean having to do without your favourite dishes. In many cases a dish designed as an accompaniment can even be transformed into a main course. Simply increase the amount of vegetables, herbs and other ingredients if you prefer plant products to meat products, to produce a balanced vegetarian meal. This applies just as much to Asparagus Ragoût with Broccoli or Tommato and Potato Stew as it does to appetising Mixed Vegetables in Coconut Milk.

Fennel and Pears
(see recipe on page 122)

LEEK AND CARROT MEDLEY

SERVES 4 ■
Preparation and cooking time: 40 minutes
Kcal per portion: 135
P = 2g, F = 12g, C = 6g

3 medium leeks (about
    500g/1lb2oz)
3 medium carrots (200g/7oz)
3 tbsps olive oil
salt and white pepper
125ml/4 fl oz strong chicken
    stock
juice of ½ lemon
1 tbsp chopped parsley

1. Remove the roots from the leeks. Halve lengthways, wash thoroughly under run-

> **TIP**
> *This also tastes delicious cold. Yoghurt flavoured with garlic can be served with it, if desired.*

ning water and cut into 1cm/½ inch pieces. Scrub or scrape the carrots. Slice first lengthways, then cut into narrow strips about 5cm/2 inches long.
2. Heat the oil in a large flameproof casserole. Fry the leeks over a medium heat until golden. Season with salt and pepper and pour in the stock. Cover and simmer for about 10 minutes over a low heat.
3. Stir in the carrot and cook for about 15-20 minutes.
4. Season the vegetables with lemon juice and, if necessary, more salt and pepper. Sprinkle with parsley.
An accompaniment to any meat dish.

CARROTS WITH SHERRY

SERVES 2 ■
Preparation and cooking time: 30 minutes
Kcal per portion: 220
P = 3g, F = 15g, C = 9g

1 bunch young carrots with
    leaves
1 shallot
20g/¾oz butter
salt and white pepper
3 tbsps dry sherry
20g/¾oz pine nuts

1. Remove the leaves from the carrots reserving a few small ones. Scrub and finely slice the carrots. Finely dice the shallot.
2. Heat the butter in a small flameproof casserole. Sweat the shallot over a medium heat until transparent. Add the sliced carrot and brown lightly, stirring constantly. Add salt, then pour in the sherry. Cover and cook over a medium heat. The vegetables should still be firm.
3. Meanwhile dry-fry the pine nuts in a small frying-pan. Finely chop the carrot leaves.
4. Season the carrots with pepper. Sprinkle with carrot leaves and pine nuts.
An accompaniment to roast chicken or braised veal.

SHALLOTS AND PEAS

SERVES 2 ■
Preparation and cooking time: 45 minutes
Kcal per portion: 195
P = 8g, F = 9g, C = 21g

250g/8oz shallots
20g/¾oz butter
½ tsp sugar
6 tbsps strong chicken stock
200g/7oz fresh shelled peas
salt and white pepper
1 tbsp chopped parsley

1. Heat the butter in a flameproof casserole. Quarter the shallots, put in the pan and sprinkle with sugar. Glaze, stirring constantly, over a low heat until golden brown. Pour in the stock, cover, and simmer for about 10 minutes.
2. When the shallots have become syrupy and are almost cooked, add the peas. Season with salt and pepper. Cook for about 5 minutes over a low heat. Serve sprinkled with parsley. frozen peas can be used instead of fresh peas.
An accompaniment to veal ragoût or braised chicken.

FRENCH BEANS WITH BLACK OLIVES

SERVES 4 ■
Preparation and cooking time: 40 minutes
Kcal per portion: 215
P = 5g, F = 12g, C = 16g

750g/1½lbs young French
    beans
4 small shallots
2 tbsps olive oil
2 thyme sprigs
salt and pepper
125ml/4 fl oz dry white wine
50g/2oz stoned black olives
2 tbsps chopped parsley

1. Snip the ends off the beans and wash. Leave small

> **TIP**
> *The cooking time depends on the size and tenderness of the beans. Always test their crispness during cooking.*

beans whole, snap larger ones in half. Chop or quarter the shallots.
2. Heat the olive oil in a flameproof casserole and brown the shallots. Add the beans and thyme sprigs. Season with salt and pepper and pour in the white wine. Cover and simmer over a medium heat. After about 5 minutes stir in the olive halves, then cook until the beans are done but still firm.
3. Discard the thyme and sprinkle with parsley.
An accompaniment to lamb chops or roast lamb.

ASPARAGUS RAGOÛT
WITH BROCCOLI

ASPARAGUS RAGOÛT WITH BROCCOLI

SERVES 4 ■

*Preparation and cooking
time: 50 minutes
Kcal per portion: 195
P = 5g, F = 18g, C = 5g*

*500g/1lb2oz white asparagus
250g/8oz broccoli
salt and white pepper
pinch of sugar
30g/1oz butter
125ml/5 fl oz single cream
1 tsp flour
pinch of cayenne pepper
a little grated lemon zest
lemon juice to taste
1 egg yolk
1 tbsp finely chopped chives*

Peel the asparagus and divide the broccoli into florets.

1. Carefully peel the asparagus spears. If necessary, cut off the ends, then chop.

Thicken the asparagus sauce with beaten egg yolk.

> **TIP**
>
> *A light meal can be produced by mixing cooked peeled prawns with the vegetables.*

Wash the broccoli and divide into small florets. Finely chop the stalks.
2. Bring a generous amount of water to the boil, containing salt, sugar and 10g/¼oz butter. Boil the asparagus for about 10-15 minutes, depending on the thickness of the spears, so that they are still firm. Boil the broccoli florets and stalk pieces in boiling salted water. They should still be firm.
3. Drain the asparagus spears and reserve the water. Measure out 500ml/16 fl oz of the asparagus cooking water. Mix with the cream and cook over medium heat until reduced by half.

Mix the cooked vegetables into the sauce.

4. Knead the remaining butter with the flour. Using a whisk, beat this into the boiling asparagus stock to thicken it. Cook for a few minutes over a high heat. Season with salt, pepper, cayenne, lemon zest and lemon juice.
5. Add the asparagus and the well-drained broccoli to the sauce. Whisk the egg yolk with a little sauce and use to thicken the ragoût. If necessary, season again, then sprinkle with chives.
An accompaniment to pork escalopes.

CHICORY IN ORANGE BUTTER

SERVES 4 ■

*Preparation and cooking
time: 30 minutes
Kcal per portion: 85
P = 2g, F = 6g, C = 5g*

*4 heads chicory (each
125g/5oz)
30g/1oz butter
1 tsp sugar
juice and grated zest of 1
orange
salt
cayenne pepper
a few mint leaves
orange segments to garnish
(optional)*

1. Remove limp outer leaves from the chicory and cut the heads in half. Remove the bitter cores.

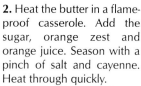

> **TIP**
>
> *With only 30 calories per 100g chicory is an extremely low-calorie vegetable, although rich in minerals. Its slightly bitter taste is pleasantly reduced by the addition of orange juice.*

2. Heat the butter in a flameproof casserole. Add the sugar, orange zest and orange juice. Season with a pinch of salt and cayenne. Heat through quickly.
3. Toss the chicory halves in the orange butter. Cover and cook, cut surfaces down, for about 10 minutes. Baste with the braising juices from time to time.
4. Serve garnished with orange segments if desired. An accompaniment to veal or turkey steaks.

Remove the limp leaves from the chicory.

Carefully cut the bitter core from the chicory halves.

Toss the chicory halves in the orange butter.

CUCUMBER WITH FISH STUFFING

SERVES 2 ■ ■
*Preparation and cooking
time: 45 minutes
Kcal per portion: 200
P = 23g, F = 4g, C = 4g*

*1 medium cucumber (about
  600g/1¼lbs)
salt and white pepper
250g/8oz cod fillet
1 egg white
1 tbsp crème fraîche
2 tbsps finely chopped dill
pinch of cayenne pepper
juice of ½ lemon
125ml/4 fl oz strong fish stock*

1. Partially peel the cucumber, leaving green stripes behind. Cut into four pieces, about 6cm/2½ inches long. Hollow them out and sprin-

TIP

*If you wish to
serve a sauce
with the
cucumber,
thicken the fish
stock with crème
fraîche.*

kle inside and outside with salt. Finely dice the remaining cucumber.
2. For the fish stuffing, cut the fish into pieces and blend well in a liquidiser. Thoroughly mix in the egg white, crème fraîche and 1 tablespoon dill. Season with salt, pepper, cayenne and lemon juice.
3. Stuff the cucumber pieces with the mixture. Place in a steamer and arrange the diced cucumber around them.
4. Pour the fish stock into the base of the saucepan. Place the steamer over the stock. Cover and steam for about 10 minutes. Serve sprinkled with dill.

TOMATO AND POTATO STEW

SERVES 4 ■
*Preparation and cooking
time: 50 minutes
Kcal per portion: 255
P = 8g, F = 12g, C = 30g*

*1 onion
1-2 garlic cloves
500g/1lb2oz beefsteak
  tomatoes
2 tbsps olive oil
1 sprig thyme
1 sprig rosemary
salt and pepper
500g/1lb2oz floury potatoes
8 tbsps chicken stock
1 tbsp chopped parsley
1 tbsp chopped basil*

1. Finely dice the onion and garlic. Blanch, peel, core and chop the tomatoes.
2. Heat the oil in a flameproof casserole and lightly brown the onion and garlic. Add the tomatoes, thyme and rosemary. Season with salt and pepper. Cover and cook over a low heat for about 5 minutes.
3. Meanwhile wash and finely dice the potatoes. Stir into the tomato mixture and pour over the stock. Cover and cook over a low heat for about 30 minutes, stirring from time to time. Season again and serve sprinkled with parsley and basil.
An accompaniment to rissoles or fried chops.

SPICY MIXED PEPPERS

SERVES 4 ■
*Preparation and cooking
time: 40 minutes
Kcal per portion: 185
P = 5g, F = 9g, C = 16g*

*2 green peppers
2 red peppers
1 Spanish onion
2 garlic cloves
4 anchovy fillets
2 tbsps olive oil
salt and pepper
½ tsp herbes de provence
125ml/4 fl oz dry white wine
100g/4oz canned sweetcorn
2 tbsps chopped parsley*

1. Wash and halve the peppers; remove the cores and seeds. Chop the halves into small squares. Dice the onion and garlic; finely chop the anchovies.
2. Heat the oil in a large nonstick frying-pan. Lightly brown the anchovies and garlic. Gradually add the vegetables, stirring constantly, and cook over a medium heat for a few minutes. Season with salt and pepper and sprinkle with the herbs. Pour in the wine. Cover and cook over a low heat for about 15-20 minutes, stirring from time to time.
3. Stir in the sweetcorn and bring to the boil over a high heat. Stir in the parsley just before serving.
An accompaniment to quick-fried meat.

SWEET AND SOUR BEETROOT

SERVES 2 ■
*Preparation and cooking
time: 50 minutes
Kcal per portion: 230
P = 2g, F = 15g, C = 14g*

*400g/14oz raw beetroot
4 small shallots
2 tbsps oil
1 tsp coriander seeds
salt and white pepper
1 tbsp maple syrup
1 tbsp balsamic vinegar
5 tbsps red wine
a few coriander sprigs*

1. Wash and peel the beetroot. Cut into 5-mm/¼ inch slices, then into strips. Quarter the shallots.
2. Heat the oil in a flameproof casserole and brown the shallot quarters.

TIP

*Beetroot is also
delicious served
with cold creamy
yoghurt or
soured cream.
When buying be
sure to get the
raw vegetable, as
beetroot is often
sold pre-cooked
for use in salads.*

3. Add the beetroot and crushed coriander seeds. Season with salt and pepper. Pour in the maple syrup, balsamic vinegar and red wine. Stir well, cover and cook for about 20-30 minutes.
4. Serve sprinkled with individual coriander leaves.
An accompaniment to boiled beef or sweetcorn rissoles.

OYSTER MUSHROOMS WITH TOMATOES

SERVES 2 ■
Preparation and cooking time: 25 minutes
Kcal per portion: 220
P = 4g, F = 16g, C = 12g

300g/10oz oyster mushrooms
1 small onion
1 garlic clove
2 tbsps oil
salt and pepper
1 sprig oregano
4 tbsps dry white wine
2 beefsteak tomatoes
1 tbsp chopped parsley or basil

1. Cut the ends off the oyster mushrooms. Wipe, pat dry and divide into pieces. Finely dice the onion and garlic.
2. Heat the oil in a non-stick frying-pan. Lightly brown the onion and garlic. Add the mushrooms and sweat for a few minutes, turning them in the oil. Sprinkle with salt,

> **TIP**
>
> *Lay slices of Mozzarella over the cooked vegetables and cover for a few minutes to melt the cheese.*

pepper and individual oregano leaves. Pour in the wine, cover and cook over a low heat for about 10 minutes.
3. Meanwhile blanch and peel the tomatoes. Dice finely, without the stalk ends or core. Scatter over the mushrooms and heat briefly. Serve sprinkled with herbs.

SAVOY CABBAGE ROLLS WITH CHANTERELLE MUSHROOMS

SERVES 2 ■ ■
Preparation and cooking time: 45 minutes
Kcal per portion: 260
P = 16g, F = 17g, C = 8g

4 large clean Savoy cabbage leaves
salt and pepper
250g/8oz chanterelle mushrooms
1 shallot
20g/¾oz butter
150g/5½oz quark or curd cheese
2 tbsps chopped herbs (basil, parsley, chervil)
30g/1oz Cheddar cheese, grated
125ml/4 fl oz chicken stock
1 tbsp soured cream

1. Blanch the cabbage leaves in plenty of boiling salted water for a few minutes. Remove from the water using a slotted spoon. Plunge briefly into ice-cold water, then drain.
2. Wipe the mushrooms and halve larger ones if necessary. Dice the shallot finely. Heat the butter in a non-stick frying-pan and fry the shallot until transparent. Add the mushrooms and brown lightly, stirring constantly.
3. Let the mushrooms cool slightly. Heat the oven to 200°C/400°F/Gas Mark 6.
4. Mix together the quark or curd cheese, herbs and cheese. Add the mushrooms. Season generously with salt and pepper.
5. Spread out the Savoy cabbage leaves. Spread over the mushroom mixture. Fold both sides of each leaf over the stuffing. Roll up from end to end and put side by side in a baking dish. Pour over the stock, cover and cook for about 25 minutes. Ten minutes before the end of the

After cooling, stir the browned mushrooms and shallots into the herb and quark mixture.

Spread the mushroom and quark mixture over the Savoy cabbage leaves. Fold the long edges inwards, then roll up.

cooking time remove the lid, spoon the juices over the rolls and brush with the soured cream.
If fresh chanterelles are unavailable, ceps or button mushrooms can be used.
An accompaniment to game. Can also be served on its own as a starter or a vegetarian main course. In the latter case double the quantities.

SPRING ONIONS WITH MUSHROOMS

SERVES 2 ■
Preparation and cooking time: 35 minutes
Kcal per portion: 185
P = 4g, F = 18g, C = 2g

1 bunch spring onions
250g/8oz button mushrooms
1 tbsp sesame oil
salt and white pepper
generous pinch of ground lemon grass
generous pinch of ground coriander
generous pinch of ground turmeric
1-2 tbsps soy sauce
a few coriander sprigs

1. Trim and wash the spring onions. Chop into thin, diagonal slices, including some of the green parts. Wipe and finely slice the mushrooms.
2. Heat the oil in a wok or

> **TIP**
>
> *If you like ethnic cooking, you should have coriander in your herb garden. It thrives well and adds an interesting flavour to many dishes.*

high-sided frying-pan. Stir-fry the onions briefly.
3. Add the mushrooms, salt and pepper. Sprinkle with the spices. Stir-fry until the vegetables are cooked but still firm. Season with the soy sauce and serve garnished with coriander sprigs.
An accompaniment to fried fish or turkey steaks.

GOLDEN CAULIFLOWER

SERVES 2 ■

Preparation and cooking time: 35 minutes
Kcal per portion: 245
P = 5g, F = 20g, C = 8g

1 small cauliflower (about 500g/1lb2oz)
1 onion
1 garlic clove
1 dried chilli
2 tbsps oil
1 tsp curry powder
generous pinch of ground saffron
salt and white pepper
3 tbsps rice wine or dry sherry
100g/4oz Greek yoghurt
a few chervil sprigs

1. Trim the cauliflower and divide into small florets. Finely dice the onion and garlic. De-seed and finely dice the chilli.
2. Heat the oil in a wok or high-sided frying-pan and sweat the onion and garlic

> **TIP**
>
> *To make a light, exotic meal, mix prawns into this dish.*

until transparent. Add the chilli, curry powder and saffron and fry briefly.
3. Add the cauliflower florets and season with salt and pepper. Cook over a medium heat, stirring constantly, until golden. Pour in the rice wine or sherry. Cover and cook over a low heat for about 10 minutes, stirring from time to time.
4. Stir the yoghurt until smooth and mix into the vegetables. Sprinkle with chervil.
An accompaniment to white fish or fried scampi.

MIXED VEGETABLES IN COCONUT MILK

SERVES 4 ■

Preparation and cooking time: 45 minutes
Kcal per portion: 160
P = 5g, F = 12g, C = 8g

4 small shallots
1 garlic clove
3 celery stalks
2 small carrots
100g/4oz mushrooms
150g/5½oz Chinese leaves
100g/4oz mange-tout
3 tbsps oil
salt and pepper
1 tsp finely grated ginger root
½ tsp ground lemon grass
generous pinch of cayenne pepper
generous pinch of sambal ulek
125ml/4 fl oz coconut milk (ready-made)
1 tbsp chopped parsley

1. Cut the shallots into wedges and finely chop the garlic. Trim and wash the other vegetables.
2. Chop the celery into thin slices. Chop the carrots, mushrooms and Chinese leaves into thin strips. Leave the mange-tout whole.
3. Heat the oil in a wok or high-sided frying-pan. Brown the vegetables, one after another, stirring constantly. Season with salt, add the spices and pour in the coconut milk. Bring to the boil and cook over a low heat for a few minutes. The vegetables should be cooked but still firm.
4. Serve sprinkled with parsley.
An accompaniment to oriental-style meat dishes.

STIR-FRIED KOHLRABI

SERVES 2 ■

Preparation and cooking time: 30 minutes
Kcal per portion: 405
P = 8g, F = 36g, C = 12g

2 medium kohlrabi (about 500g/1lb2oz)
1 small onion
2 tbsps oil
½ tsp mild curry powder
2 tbsps soy sauce
2 tbsps sunflower seeds

1. Remove any leaves from the kohlrabi and set aside. Peel the kohlrabi, slice thinly, then cut into strips. Finely dice the onion.
2. Heat the oil in a wok or high-sided frying-pan and sweat the onion until transparent. Add the strips of kohlrabi and fry gently over a medium heat, stirring constantly. Sprinkle with curry powder, pour over the soy sauce and continue to stir-fry until the kohlrabi is cooked.
3. Dry-fry the sunflower seeds in a second frying-pan.
4. Finely slice the reserved kohlrabi leaves. Sprinkle over the vegetables, with the sunflower seeds.
An accompaniment to curried chicken breast.

FRIED CELERIAC WITH SESAME SEED CRUST

SERVES 2 ■

Preparation and cooking time: 1 hour
Kcal per portion: 325
P = 25g, F = 21g, C = 12g

about 400g/14oz celeriac
1 small egg
20g/¾oz cracked wheat
30g/1oz sesame seeds
salt and white pepper
2 tbsps oil

1. Wash the celeriac; leave it whole and un-peeled. Boil for about 40 minutes in plenty of boiling salted water, until cooked but not too soft.
2. Cool the celeriac briefly in cold water, then pull off the skin or peel.
3. Chop the celeriac into 1cm/½ inch slices. Beat the egg with a fork. Combine the cracked wheat and sesame seeds. Lightly dust

> **TIP**
>
> *Cooking the celeriac in the pressure-cooker saves a great deal of time. Peel while still hot, when the skin is easier to remove.*

the celeriac slices with salt and pepper. Turn the slices first in the egg, then in the sesame seed mixture.
4. Heat the oil in a large non-stick frying-pan. Fry the celeriac slices over a medium heat for about 3 minutes on each side, until golden.
An accompaniment to roast venison or medallions of venison. Can also be served as a light meal with cranberries.

COURGETTE PATTIES

SERVES 4 ■

*Preparation and cooking
time: 30 minutes
Kcal per portion: 190
P = 6g, F = 16g, C = 2g*

*2 medium courgettes (about
    400g/14oz)
1 small onion
1 garlic clove
½ bunch parsley
100g/4oz Feta cheese
1 egg
salt and pepper
3 tbsps oil*

1. Wash the courgettes. Cut
off the ends and grate the
flesh coarsely.
2. Finely dice the onion and
garlic. Chop the parsley and
mash the cheese.
3. Mix all these ingredients
together. Beat the egg. Add
to the other ingredients and

TIP

*Mix some
coarsely chopped
sunflower seeds
into the mixture.*

---

mix thoroughly. Season the
mixture generously with salt
and pepper.
4. Heat the oil in a large non-
stick frying-pan. Using a
tablespoon, place small balls
of the mixture in the hot fat.
Press flat with the back of a
spoon and fry over a medium heat for about 3-4 minutes on each side. Drain on
absorbent paper and serve
immediately.
An accompaniment to roast
lamb or veal. Can also be
served as a meal for two
with rémoulade sauce.

COURGETTES STUFFED WITH CHICKEN AND PRAWNS

SERVES 4 ■

*Preparation and cooking
time: 1 hour
Kcal per portion: 230
P = 25g, F = 9g, C = 11g*

*4 medium courgettes (each
    about 200g/7oz)
1 tbsp oil
2 tbsps chopped onion
300g/10oz chicken breast
1 tbsp finely chopped dill
1 egg
1 tbsp breadcrumbs
100g/4oz cooked peeled
    prawns
salt and white pepper
1 tbsp curry powder
freshly grated ginger root
cayenne pepper
15g/½oz butter
125ml/4 fl oz strong chicken
    stock*

1. Wash the courgettes.
Halve lengthways and hol-
low out with a spoon, leaving a thin shell. Finely chop
the flesh.
2. Heat the oil in a non-stick
frying-pan. Sweat the onion
with the courgette.
3. Heat the oven to
200°C/400°F/Gas Mark 6.
4. Finely grind the chicken in
a liquidiser or food processor. Mash into a smooth
meat stuffing with the courgette mixture, dill, egg and
breadcrumbs. Stir in the
prawns. Season well with
salt, pepper, curry powder,
ginger and cayenne. Stuff
the mixture into the hol-
lowed-out courgette halves.
5. Butter a large baking dish
and put in the courgettes.
Dot the stuffing with butter
and bake for about 30 minutes. After 15 minutes, pour
over the chicken stock.

Halve the courgettes lengthways.
Hollow out and finely chop the
flesh.

Mash together the processed
chicken, fried vegetables, dill, egg
and breadcrumbs.

Mix the prawns into the meat
stuffing; add seasoning and
spices.

Fill the hollowed out courgette
halves with the chicken and
prawn mixture.

TOMATOES STUFFED WITH FETA CHEESE

SERVES 4 ■ ■

*Preparation and cooking
time: 1 hour
Kcal per portion: 145
P = 4g, F = 12g, C = 4g*

*8 medium ripe tomatoes
salt and pepper
1 onion
2 garlic cloves
1 thyme sprig
1 oregano sprig
2 parsley stalks
100g/4oz Feta cheese
1 egg
1 tbsp breadcrumbs
1-2 tbsps olive oil*

1. Cut a lid from the tomatoes and reserve. Hollow out
the tomatoes using a small
spoon. Season the insides
with salt and pepper.
2. Heat the oven to
200°C/400°F/Gas Mark 6.
3. For the stuffing, finely dice
the onion and garlic. Pull the
leaves from the thyme and
oregano. Finely chop,
together with the parsley.
Mash the Feta with a fork or
blend in a liquidiser. Add the
egg and the breadcrumbs.
Mix to a smooth paste with
the other ingredients. If necessary, season with salt and
pepper.
4. Stuff the tomatoes with
the mixture and cover with
the lids. Brush a small baking
dish with some of the oil. Put
in the tomatoes and brush
with the remaining oil. Cook
in the centre of the oven for
about 25-30 minutes.
Accompaniment:
green salad and unpeeled
boiled potatoes. Can also be
served cold as a starter.

FENNEL AND PEARS

(see photo on page 108)

SERVES 2 ■
Preparation and cooking time: 35 minutes
Kcal per portion: 260
P = 6g, f = 9g, C = 28g

2 small fennel bulbs (about 300g/10oz)
2 pears
juice of ½ lemon
20g/¾oz butter or margarine
salt and white pepper
cayenne pepper
125ml/4 fl oz dry white wine
50g/2oz shelled peas

1. Wash and trim the fennel bulbs. Cut off and reserve any green leaves. Halve and thinly slice the bulbs. Peel, halve and core the pears.

TIP

The pears used for this dish should not be too soft.

Slice the halves lengthways and sprinkle with lemon juice.
2. Heat the butter or margarine in a flameproof casserole. Fry the fennel strips lightly. Season with salt, pepper and a pinch of cayenne; pour in the wine. Cover and simmer for about 15 minutes.
3. Add the pear slices and peas. Cover and cook for just a few minutes.
4. Finely chop the reserved fennel leaves and sprinkle over the vegetables.
An accompaniment to Italian-style braised veal.

The fennel leaves can be used for garnishing.

Thinly slice the fennel bulbs and the pears.

Add the pear slices and peas to the braised strips of fennel.

CELERY WITH MOZZARELLA

SERVES 4 ■
Preparation and cooking time: 1 hour
Kcal per portion: 245
P = 5g, F = 9g, C = 16g

2 heads celery (each about 400g/14oz)
30g/1oz butter
salt and white pepper
125ml/4 fl oz dry white wine
4 beefsteak tomatoes
10 stoned black olives
6-8 basil leaves
100g/4oz Mozzarella cheese

1. Cut the bottom and any green leaves from the celery. Cut in half lengthways.
2. Heat the butter in a large flameproof casserole. Turn the celery halves in the butter, season with salt and pepper and pour in the wine. Cover and simmer gently for about 20 minutes.
3. Meanwhile blanch, peel, core and finely dice the tomatoes. Slice the olives and cut the basil leaves into thin strips. Combine with the diced tomato. Season with salt and pepper. Cut the Mozzarella into thin slices.
4. Heat the grill to medium.
5. Turn the celery over so that the cut surfaces face upward. Cover with the tomato mixture, then with cheese. Brown under the grill for 10 minutes.
An accompaniment to fillet steak or rissoles. Can be served with mashed potato as a vegetarian main course for two.

SPINACH WITH YOGHURT

SERVES 4 ■
Preparation and cooking time: 35 minutes
Kcal per portion: 90
P = 3g, F = 8g, C = 2g

500g/1lb2oz young spinach
1 onion
2-3 garlic cloves
2 tbsps oil
1 small dried chilli
a little freshly grated ginger root
1 tsp curry powder
salt and white pepper
175g/6oz Greek yoghurt
tomato strips to garnish

1. Trim the spinach and remove the thicker stalks. Thoroughly wash the leaves several times and drain.
2. Finely dice the onion and one garlic clove. Heat the oil in a wok or high-sided frying-pan. Sweat the onion and garlic until transparent.
3. De-seed and finely chop the chilli. Add to the pan with the grated ginger and curry powder. Lightly brown over a medium heat. Stir in the spinach leaves, cover and leave for a few minutes until they collapse.
4. Meanwhile crush the remaining garlic cloves and mix with the yoghurt. Season generously with salt and pepper.
5. Arrange the spinach in rings on warmed plates. Pour the garlic yoghurt into the centre. If desired, sprinkle with a little curry powder, toasted almonds or pistachio nuts. Garnish with thin strips of tomato.
An accompaniment to grilled kebabs.

Index